A YEAR IN A DITCH

Published by
Whittles Publishing,
Dunbeath,
Caithness KW6 6EG,
Scotland, UK

www.whittlespublishing.com

© 2016 J C Jeremy Hobson

ISBN 978-184995-164-7

Printed by Melita Press, Malta

A YEAR IN A DITCH

J C JEREMY HOBSON

Whittles Publishing

CONTENTS

ACKNOWLEDGEMENTS

A great number of individuals and organisations helped in the compilation of this book, so to acknowledge one would risk offending others. I therefore offer grateful thanks to all.

Any lengthy quotes have been taken from books which are out of copyright, or are otherwise in the public domain. In other instances, and in accordance with my understanding of the UK's copyright laws, I have not necessarily sought out permission to quote minor extracts taken from books, magazines and the internet where they amounted to merely a few words – but can assure anyone concerned that I have not taken any quote and used it out of context … nor to the detriment of what was intended by the author. I have also, on every occasion, credited the author and identified the publication. However, should anyone reading the text feel that I should have done more, I can only offer my apologies and ask them to contact either myself or the publisher in order that amends can be made in any future reprints.

As far as photographs are concerned, unless there is credit given alongside, it should be assumed they are my own. Particular thanks must, though, be given to Helen Tait-Wright, Phil Rant, Kirsteen Atkinson and Philip Watts – and to the wonderful photo-sourcing opportunities afforded by Wikimedia Commons (www.commons.wikimedia.org).

INTRODUCTION

Don't you just love technical and legal jargon?! Apparently, for certain statutory purposes – and certainly according to the Water Resources Act 1991, the word 'watercourse' encompasses and includes all 'rivers, streams, ditches, drains, cuts, culverts, dykes, sluices, sewers and passages through which water flows except mains and other pipes…'. Furthermore (pay attention at the back; there may be questions later!), although this general description of a watercourse includes ditches, 'for purposes relating to the restoration and improvement of ditches the definition of "ditch" includes a culverted and piped ditch but does not include a watercourse vested in or under the control of a drainage body'.

However, that's enough of that. Far more prosaic is the observation that man-made ditches of one form or another have threaded their way through the British countryside for millennia. Sometimes straight, sometimes meandering, they are essential in ensuring that water passes from its source and eventually to the sea with the minimum of disruption and damage to the surrounding land. As the 18th century poet William Cowper said of the River Ouse – and it applies equally to a good number of other water routes:

> Here Ouse, slow winding through the level plain
> Of spacious meads, with cattle sprinkled o'er,
> Conducts the eye along his sinuous course
> Delighted.

Most commonly seen as a simple yet effective way of keeping land drained and water on the move, there are, however (as the Water Resources Act so jargonistically suggests!), several types of ditches and waterways, the most usual of which are the open sort that form an integral part of most drainage systems and simply intercept and collect water from surrounding areas – or act as receivers and carriers of water from an underground drainage system. Their purpose is to move water quickly along but, as has been seen in recent winters, ditches do not always do that good a job – most usually, it must be admitted, as a result of neglect or human interference.

As with so many things, ditches were initially devised and developed for a time when there were far fewer people around than there are nowadays – and for a period when the rural population far outweighed any confined, urban living. The mid-1800s (the first point ever when 'town' dwellers outnumbered those who lived and worked in the countryside) saw huge changes. Planners and civil engineers diverted natural streams underground – into which they initially fed both surplus water and sanitation without any thought as to what might be the eventual result once it ceased to be their immediate responsibility.

MORE PONG THAN POETRY

Even before the mid-1800s, the Fleet river (which still runs underground through part of modern-day London) was, by 1749, frequently referred to as the 'Fleet Ditch' and had already become not much more than an open sewer – the contents of which were described by well-known writers and poets of the time. Alexander Pope mentioned a 'large tribute of dead dogs' and Jonathan Swift commented that the 'sweepings from butchers' stalls, dung, guts and blood, drown'd puppies, stinking sprats, all drench'd in mud, dead cats and turnip-tops, come tumbling down the flood'. And we think we have problems with pollution on occasion!

FROM SOURCE TO SEA... OR LEVEE

Heavy rainfall obviously has to go somewhere – in urban situations much has been blamed on the fact that many houses have a concrete or paved parking area in what was once the garden and so it is nowadays impossible for water to drain away naturally into the permeable soil. Instead it finds its way into culverts or roadside drains ill-designed to cope with the added capacity. It might or might not eventually continue its journey to the sea via streams and rivers and in doing so, adds considerably to the surplus water collected en route from rural areas in man-made ditches designed only to pick up run-off from surrounding farmland. Without due care and attention all along its journey from source to sea, it is not surprising that flooding occurs.

The neglect of ditches is seen by some as being a reason for recent and very serious problems in Britain. It was certainly the case in America when 'Hurricane Katrina' caused the ditches there to over-top and spill water onto vast tracts of surrounding land. As something of an 'aside' but of interest nevertheless, whilst alternative names for ditches and dykes in the UK are explained in the following chapter, it is well worth noting here that, in the US, ditches are sometimes referred to as 'levees' – as evidenced by the Led Zeppelin 1971 song, When The Levee Breaks. They were, of course, further immortalised in music by Don McLean later in the same year when he released American Pie and famously drove his 'Chevy to the levee, but the levee was dry...'.

Coping with flood water. This roadside ditch is struggling to cope with the overflow from the River Thames – the field adjacent being completely under water. (Photo: David Collins)

ALL THINGS TO ALL MEN... AND WILDLIFE

Not *all* ditches were, however, intended to convey water and drain the land. Some have been constructed throughout the ages for a variety of purposes, not the least common of which was as a farming barrier. In places such as Dartmoor, for example, in the 13th century, areas of moorland grazing were separated from enclosed lands by corn ditches comprising a ditch and a vertical stone-faced bank intended to prevent livestock from entering cultivated fields. Similarly, but in relatively more recent times, landscape gardeners like 'Capability' Brown created the 'ha-ha' – a carefully designed and landscaped dry ditch and retaining wall built so as not to obstruct the view across the parkland from a stately home or magnificent country pile. As to how they got their name, Horace Walpole, writing in 1780, claimed that 'The common people called them "Ha! Ha's" to express their surprise at finding a sudden and unperceived check to their walk'.

It is not too dramatic to state that the more conventional type of water-filled ditch is yet another of Britain's threatened 'species'. They have undoubtedly become less numerous (due in no small part to the trend of 'agri-business' in the late 20th century whereby open waterways were piped underground in order to allow more potential profit on the surface), while those that do survive are rapidly deteriorating in quality because of a range of issues, including agricultural pollution, unsuitable water level management and 'managed retreat' schemes on the coastline.

As I rapidly came to realise when I began researching for this book, the subject of ditches as a means of drainage cannot be taken in isolation. While flooding is an undesirable occurrence in most situations, conversely, the *deliberate* flooding of water meadows in southern England in order to improve summer grazing for cattle and sheep (particularly sheep) also required a clever and essential network of channels through which water from a main river could be diverted for the good of the land.

The deliberate flooding of water meadows in southern England in order to improve summer grazing for sheep required a clever network of channels through which water from a main river could be diverted for the good of the land.

A ditch and its immediate surroundings offers wildlife a safe 'corridor': safe nesting and a ready food source for birds, and the perfect environment for water or marsh-loving plants.

Ditches are also, almost incidentally, but very importantly, a literal life-line for many species of flora and fauna – and may even form wildlife 'corridors' along which otherwise vulnerable animals and birds can travel with the minimum risk of predation. They provide sheltered nesting sites for wild duck and game birds and, if the ditch runs along the base of a hedgerow, there is plenty of additional cover in which song birds can hide, feed and produce fledglings during the summer months. Hares may choose the vegetation along a ditch bank to create a daytime 'form' in which to rest – and rabbits will certainly avail themselves of such sanctuary. A ditch and its immediate environment is also vital for the survival of damselflies, dragonflies, butterflies and all manner of insects, winged or not. Along the banks grow many native grasses and flowers and, in the water itself, there are likely to be an inordinate number of oxygenating plants, plus threatened invertebrates such as the Fen raft spider, lesser water-measurer and shining ram's-horn snail. Another rare water-beetle which I include as much for its delightful name as for its rarity and the fact that it is one of the species mentioned in the Biodiversity Action Plan (BAP) is the one-grooved diving beetle.

Hidden depths

Ditches are, when you think about it, just like us – at times sluggish, or with hidden depths; on other occasions sparkling and full of life. They are sometimes dry, sometimes simply full of rubbish! Furthermore,

EXPLAINING THE BIODIVERSITY ACTION PLAN

Both fauna and flora are included in the Biodiversity Action Plan, which was originally created during the years 1995–1999 in order to monitor 'priority species and habitats… identified as being the most threatened and requiring conservation action'.

The initial lists were subsequently updated in 2007 following a two-year review. This was the first such review of the lists and provided an opportunity to take into account emerging new priorities, conservation successes, and the huge amount of new information that had been gathered since the original lists were created.

Selection of priority species and habitats for the priority lists followed consideration by expert working groups against a set of selection criteria, based on rapid decline, high risk, and habitats of importance for key species. Following the review, the number of priority species increased from less than 600 to 1,150, and the number of priority habitats increased from 49 to 65.

In 2012, the UK Post-2010 Biodiversity Framework superseded the original UK Biodiversity Action Plan – but the initial lists of priority species and habitats remain important and valuable reference sources and have been of considerable use in helping to draw up statutory lists of priorities in areas of the British Isles.

whilst they might possibly not feature in your everyday thinking, their importance is seemingly hidden away in the human brain. According to analysts who specialise in such things, 'to dream of falling in a ditch denotes degradation and personal loss; but if you jump over it, you will live down any suspicion of wrong-doing'.

At the Manchester Art Gallery hangs a painting by Ford Madox Brown. Entitled *Work* (and painted between 1852 and 1865), depicted at the very centre of the piece are a pair of ditch-diggers – apparently chosen as subjects by the artist in order to perfectly exemplify 'the virility, strength and diligence forming the foundation of an ethical society'. The Bible makes several references to ditches – as does Dante Alighieri in the first part of his epic *Divine Comedy*, whilst actor Liam Neeson, as a means of keeping himself grounded, is quoted as saying: 'I never forget where I'm from. Whenever I pass a building site or see somebody digging a ditch, I always think, "That's real work"'.

The ditch appears in many well-known sayings, just a few of which include 'die in the last ditch'; 'last ditch attempt'; 'dull as ditch-water', and 'looks like he/she slept in a ditch'. 'Leg in the ditch' might be called out to a child who stumbles (possibly whilst skipping with a rope) and 'in a ditch' could indicate the state of mind of someone either drunk or unsure of what to do next. The Dutch have a traditional warning: 'Don't walk in seven ditches all at the same time', meaning do all you can to avoid getting into trouble (presumably, because much of the country is low-lying: the ditches will more often than not be full of water – and who knows what hidden depth or danger lurks below the surface). Some American

In America, pheasants are sometimes referred to as 'ditch chickens'. (Photo: nottsexminer/Wikimedia Commons)

hunters refer to the pheasant as a 'ditch chicken' due to its love of marshy places, whilst a slow or stupid person might be rather unkindly referred to as being as 'thick as a ditch'. Then, of course, there is the very everyday almost universal use of 'ditch' to indicate that one is discarding something or someone.

'Ploughed land... and gleaming dykes'

The humble ditch is even included in the diary entries of the likes of First World War poet Siegfried Sassoon who, during a quiet spell in December 1915, recorded the following:

> ... Tried to make black pony jump a ditch and failed utterly. Saw a heron, which sailed slowly away across the misty flats of ploughed land, grey, still evening, gleaming dykes, willows and poplars; a few lights here and there as we rode home, and flicker of star shells in the sky beyond...

In war as well as peacetime, it was, then, obviously quite possible to see something of beauty in a 'gleaming dyke' and to appreciate and notice whatever wildlife and natural habitat might be present.

A century on from when Sassoon pencilled his observations, I hope to show something of how ditches have fared in the interim: their importance in preventing future flooding; and what steps are being taken to ensure their survival – and the survival of the plants, reptiles and animals that currently frequent these places. In amongst the most serious of observations there is, nonetheless, room to include the more quirky snippets – the fanciful and factual, and even just how ditches are an integral part of some very strange sports and pastimes indeed!

Most crucially, however, it is my utmost wish that my enthusiasm and concerns for ditches and the important role they have in today's environment will be understood by anyone and everyone with an interest in the countryside past, present and future. As was once said (the source sadly unattributable): 'A walk amongst nature, whether by the sea, river, hill, valley, meadow or wood, works wonders for the human spirit.'

Such walks cannot, though, be fully enjoyed without a little knowledge – and also an awareness of the fact that nature, as managed by human intervention for whatever purpose, can be so easily unbalanced. At one point in our history, the length of time between a heavy fall of rain and its subsequent effects on springs and water levels was something of a mystery to our ancestors, and any sudden unexpected flooding after a period of dry weather was thought to portend disaster – and was, on occasions, referred to as 'woe-water' because, according to one 15th century writer, its arrival 'presaged sorrow to come'. The reasons were, of course, the time rain water took to travel through the soil and sub-strata before reappearing. Nowadays there is no such space of time due to the fact that land is drained and there are fewer naturally occurring places for water to linger before percolating onwards. Such boggy corners, ponds and slow-running ditches therefore need conserving and maintaining.

Columnist and author Simon Barnes, writing in *The Times* in April 2013, summed up the situation brilliantly when he observed that: 'A living countryside is not a luxury but a necessity for the human population; if you let conservation go hang until your pockets are jingling there will be a lot less to conserve.'

1

A BRIEF **HISTORY** OF DITCHES

One particular dictionary definition of a ditch describes it as being 'a narrow passage to carry water away' and a dyke as 'a wall or bank built to keep flood water back and prevent flooding' (behind which there may, or may not, be a drain). It does, though, greatly depend on where you are in Britain as in some areas the word 'dyke' is used by locals to describe a drainage ditch! Even more confusingly, it appears that, many centuries ago, a dyke had nothing at all to do with water and it was the 'wall or bank' part of the dictionary definition, which was used to defend ancient settlers from marauding invaders intent on conquest, rape, pillage or just about anything else that might have constituted a good day's entertainment of the era. Such structures are most commonly known as 'war dykes'.

WAR **DYKES**

Archaeologists sometimes refer to these battle defences as being 'prehistoric linear boundary earthworks' which, though a bit of a mouthful, does, I suppose, explain much of what they are and the period of history when many were constructed. In East Anglia can still be seen Fleam Dyke and Heydon Ditch whilst elsewhere in the country are places such as Dane's Dyke, Scot's Dyke and possibly the most famous of all, Offa's Dyke.

Not all were constructed at the same time and many were added to, or rebuilt, at various periods. Some defensive dykes, particularly in East Anglia, were, so archaeologists believe, begun in the Iron Age and modified in Anglo-Saxon times. Built as a ditch and a bank (the bank obviously being formed by the spoil dug from the ditch), and sometimes topped-off by a stockade or hedgerow planting, parts of the Fleam Dyke are even now – ditch and bank combined – around nine metres deep. Taking into account erosion and subsequent soil build-up at their base during the ensuing centuries, what Herculean efforts must have been put into the original construction?

It would appear that the Romans had no use for such defences (unless one counts Hadrian's Wall as being a 'war dyke') but after the Norman Conquest, the principle of digging out earthworks as a defence barrier most certainly regained favour, as can be evidenced by the 'motte and bailey' system of protection.

PROTECTION OR STATUS SYMBOL?

Not all is cut and dry when it comes to discussing war dykes; similar edifices of varying sizes were actually built as much as a status symbol by important chieftains, or as a means of containing livestock. Even experienced historians are in some doubt as to what might have been the original purpose of some which can still be seen today, either as tangible structures or simply as crop-marks which can only be discerned from the air.

In Medieval times, many moats were dug around the castles and dwellings of important landowners and even surrounded religious buildings. Always consisting of wide ditches, they may or may not have been designed to be dry like war dykes, or be either permanently or seasonally water-filled. Like war dykes, they were not necessarily built with the express purpose of keeping out intruders and some were created simply as a status symbol – and occasionally dug around islands created for agriculture and horticulture (presumably to protect crops from damage by wild animals such as boar and deer, or domestic livestock).

Whatever the reason, a National Trust website states that around 6,000 moated sites can still be identified, most of which were constructed between 1250 and 1350. The greatest concentration is seemingly found in central and eastern parts of England but ditches built as moats are, nevertheless, 'widely scattered throughout England and exhibit a high level of diversity in their forms and sizes'.

ENTRENCHED IN MUDDY DITCHES

Unlike Basil Fawlty in television's *Fawlty Towers*, it's impossible not to 'mention the war' when it comes to the subject of ditches. What were the First World War trenches if not ditches? They were, though, obviously dug for the soldiers' protection rather than as passageways for water. That, at least, was the theory but in practice, on the British side anyway, they often became muddy and water-logged due to military strategy and topographical factors.

The remains of a 500 BC (Iron Age) war
dyke on Stockbridge Down, Hampshire.

With a good view of the surrounding countryside from the top, steep
(man-made) banks made it more difficult for the enemy to gain hold.

As historian John Simkin (*www.sparticus-educational.com*) points out, the idea of trench warfare came originally from the German side and so they were the first to decide where to stand fast and dig – as a result of which they were able to choose the best places in which to build their trenches. As Simkin explains: 'The possession of the higher ground not only gave the Germans a tactical advantage, but it also forced the British to live in the worst conditions. Most of this area was rarely a few feet above sea level. As soon as soldiers began to dig down they would invariably find water two or three feet below the surface. Along the whole line, trench life involved a never-ending struggle against water and mud.'

C. S. Lewis, writer and author of the *Narnia* series of books, recalled his time on the Western Front during the winter months: 'weariness and water were our chief enemies… One walked in the trenches in thigh gumboots with water above the knee, and one remembers the icy stream welling up inside the boot when you punctured it on concealed barbed wire.'

American journalist Ernie Pyle was one of the most famous war correspondents of the Second World War. As part of an article entitled *Digging and Grousing* published on March 23rd, 1943, he had this to say:

The day got hot, and we took off our shirts. One sweating soldier said: 'Five years ago you couldn't a got me to dig a ditch for five dollars an hour. Now look at me.

'You can't stop me digging ditches. I don't even want pay for it; I just dig for love. And I sure do hope this digging today is all wasted effort; I never wanted to do useless work so bad in my life… and brother I ain't joking. I love to dig ditches.'

AN OVERSEAS INFLUENCE

Dykes are, arguably, best known in the Netherlands and it is no co-incidence that the word 'dyke' is more likely to be used in East Anglia than it is anywhere else due to the long-time interconnection between the two places. Between 1634 and 1655, one Cornelius Vermuyden, a Dutchman from Zeeland, was given responsibility for draining the Fens – a feat that is even now sometimes referred to as 'the greatest land reclamation in England'. The system he adopted was to make straight cuts to shorten the length of the rivers, with minor drains feeding into the main cut in

The flat land of Holland – and resultant flooding – led to a complicated nationwide system of drainage ditches and dykes.

a herring-bone pattern. But, even earlier than Vermuyden, Dutch drainage experts such as Peter Peterson (described as a 'dyke-reeve' on an inscription in Haddiscoe church) had been employed in Norfolk to improve the viability of the low-lying farmland.

The reason why the expertise of Dutch civil engineers was called upon in Britain is not difficult to see. Holland is low-lying and its topography means that it is vulnerable to the effects of the North Sea (there are only beaches and no cliffs as there are in Britain) and also the rivers of inland Europe which pass through. For countless years, the Dutch have had to cope with these factors, as a result of which the country is criss-crossed with miles and miles of dykes, ditches and canals – all of which ensure that the water is kept where it should be and will not flood precious farmland or, more importantly, housing and industry. A visit to almost any area of the Netherlands, be it urban or rural, shows a land intercepted by a great deal of water.

With a system that began in the Middle Ages when farmers used to dig out islands and stack up vegetation and unwanted debris to make a safe place on which to build a house and cultivate a few crops to ensure survival, the Dutch are now the world's experts on ditches and dykes – so much so that, after the atrocious flooding in Britain in February 2014, the UK government's Environment Agency brought in the Van Heck group and various individual Dutch civil engineers in order to avail themselves of their experience, advice and expertise.

REVOLUTION IN THE FENS

Engineers like Dutchman Cornelius Vermuyden were not popular amongst the fen-men of eastern England. Used to grazing their animals on the grassland and then, during the winter months, gaining a further food source in the fish and wildfowl that the area provided naturally, the draining of their land was seen in much the same way as the Luddites looked upon the arrival of machinery in the mills in the early decades of the 1800s. Worse was the fact that, strapped for cash, both James I and Charles I thought that, by draining the land, it would become more productive for cereal growing and other introduced crops and, rather than pay the drainage developers with coins of the realm, instead offered them land in lieu.

Understandably, this did not go down at all well with those who had previously enjoyed commoner's rights over the fenland. They responded both verbally by protesting to parliament and physically by damaging the dykes and ditches as they were being constructed. Whilst they were successful for a time, a century or so later most of the fenland had, nevertheless, been drained and enclosed and was under private ownership.

A DITCH BY ANY OTHER NAME

The fact that the Dutch influence may well be the reason why ditches are sometimes known as dykes is simple enough to understand (the Flemish word being 'dijk') but, throughout history, ditches have been given many other names depending on their purpose, region and local topography. In Anglo-Saxon times, a ditch was known as a 'dïk' so there is an obvious connection there too.

A straight, uncomplicated ditch that takes water from one place to another in the low-lying lands of Britain is sometimes called a 'culvert' – particularly when piped underground (under a road or farm entrance) for a part of its way. On the moors and uplands, small open furrows used for draining what is, at any time, relatively poor grazing, have long been known as 'grips'. To make them, tapered V-shaped channels were cut across the slope, from where the water would eventually evacuate into larger drains or natural watercourses. Purely as an aside but relevant nevertheless, open gutters and channels that occur naturally in some upland limestone rock strata, particularly in the north of England around Malham, are, if I remember my geography lessons correctly, known as 'clints' and 'grykes' depending on whether they go up and down, or from side to side.

Further north, in parts of Scotland, was developed a boundary system not dissimilar in construction to the 'war dykes' mentioned at the beginning of this chapter. There, in common farming practice at least 200 years ago, many boundaries took the form of earth banks, atop which was planted a hawthorn hedge – which was, according to the Rev. David Ure's *General View of the Agriculture in the County of Dumbarton*, written in 1794, 'planted in a horizontal direction, and immediately upon the soil side of the turf taken from the ditch; the turf or sod is laid with the grassy side uppermost, upon the old surface, now the base of the dyke'. The dyke or ditch itself was (and still is) often known as a 'clap dyke' for the very simple reason that when dug, their sides were 'clapped' hard with the back of the ditch-cutter's spade in order to make them more solid and less likely to collapse.

On the east coast of England, in Lincolnshire, a low-lying, likely-to-flood area was known as a 'carr' and for this reason a ditch or drainage channel dug to help prevent flooding was referred to as a 'carr-dyke'. Elsewhere in the county such a channel might simply be a 'drain' – and a drain dug at the base of a boundary enclosure bank, a 'delph'. Delph, to my mind at least, strikes again of a Dutch influence but, according to those who know far better, it is apparently a corruption of the Old English word 'delfan' which means 'to dig'.

Wales and Ireland also have local names for ditches, most of which mirror those of the majority of the UK; however, in Wales a ditch may possibly also be known as a 'reen' – a word derived from either the Old English 'ryne' or the Welsh 'rhewyn'. The close proximity to southern Wales is undoubtedly the reason why in Gloucestershire and Somerset such waterways are occasionally referred to as 'rhynes'.

Because of the digging out of peat as a fuel source over many generations and also the need to drain off wet and relatively poor grazing, rural Ireland has many ditches and dykes, especially in low-lying regions like County Limerick. Here, for hundreds of years, farmers have been digging ditches between their fields and flinging the result spoil to one side, thereby creating a bank – which is then sometimes topped off by dry-stone walling. It is a combination of Irish madness, a love of all things equine and the way farming practice has developed over the years (grass pasture, small fields, plenty of ditches, hedges and walls) that has made the sport of fox-hunting so popular in southern Ireland, because to jump a horse at a high wall or hedge – at the base of which lays a deep ditch – whilst at full gallop in pursuit of hounds undoubtedly gives the brave/fool-hardy rider an adrenaline boost like no other!

DITCHERS AND DROWNERS

In Britain, the local fox-hunting packs were often responsible for the cleaning out and maintaining of ditches and hedgerows – all of which helped farmers and other countrymen in keeping both in good order. Charles Willoughby, writing in his 1952 book *Come and Hunt*, remarked that many hunt committees had 'a hedging and ditching organisation… I can't quote facts and figures now, for old records are not available, but can say that the amount of hedging and ditching carried out each year by that admirable organisation was amazing'.

Not only do the ditches, dykes, drains and various water channels have specific regional and/or colloquial names derived through the ages, but so too do the men who dug, developed and maintained them. The dyke-reeve has already been mentioned but there are several more, particularly when it comes to the water meadows of southern England.

As has been pointed out, the subject of ditches cannot be taken in isolation: a ditch serves many purposes and whilst the main one is obviously to keep water moving and thus prevent flooding, there are some instances where farming practices of the past benefited from deliberate seasonal 'drowning' of the land. To do this required experts and specialists who may have been employed solely by one farmer but, far more likely, were workers who travelled from place to place in much the same way as road-menders, hedge-cutters, hop-pickers and threshers.

MEN OF THE MEADOWS

Also known as 'mead-men' or 'water-men', the 'drowners' of southern England had an important job to do; however, because the majority of

A straight, uncomplicated ditch that takes water from one place to another in the low-lying lands of Britain is sometimes called a 'culvert' – particularly when piped underground (under a road or farm entrance) for a part of its way.

them moved from place to place, they were somewhat mysterious beings and suffered some bad press in exactly the same way as the 'Bogeyman' might elsewhere have been used by parents to instil fear in their children!

Obviously done in an effort to keep them away from the many potentially dangerous waterways, southern rural youngsters were, even as late as the 1930s, told that – though they might see many pretty 'jewels' under the surface (presumably alluding to the sparkling bubbles and interestingly coloured stones which are always magnified by a clear chalk stream that always seems shallower than it is) – they shouldn't reach in to touch as, if they leant too far, the Drowner would come and get them. No wonder then that children were fearful of this particular countryside sub-contractor who was, in fact, just an ordinary person going about his designated employment!

The country writer A. G. Street wrote in his book *Farming England* (published in 1937) that:

> ... the water meadows were eagerly sought after and most carefully tended. These productive acres with their complicated system of irrigation are a feature of this downland country. Between every two downland ridges flows a river, for the

steep scarp of the Downs tilts their rainfall into the valley very swiftly. When properly tended and 'drowned' during the winter months – six weeks' water in the meadows before Christmas was the ideal aimed at by that generally cantankerous old craftsman, the drowner – the dairy herd could go out to grass, good grass, at Lady Day, and in early seasons in late February. This was a great asset to the dairy farmer, as a sufficiency of good water-meadows enabled him to produce a month's summer milk at winter price.

Maintaining the water flow in the meadows of southern England might have been the responsibility of the shepherd – or of a travelling 'drowner'.

A complicated system

It was a certain Rowland Vaughan who, in the early part of the 17th century, supposedly 'invented' the water meadow system as a result of noticing just how much earlier and lusher grass had grown where a mole had inadvertently burrowed through a riverbank. Vaughan cannot, however, take full credit as although it may well have been during this century that the practice became particularly popular, the human population has, of course, been controlling water flow for irrigation and drainage purposes worldwide for several thousand years.

'Drowning' the English meadows in Vaughan's time and onwards was a complicated, labour-intensive system which worked on the principle that plants (grass) need to grow in temperatures above five degrees centigrade. On a cold winter's day, the water from the river is usually warmer than this and the drowner's work ensured that river water could be diverted over the water meadow thus warming the grassland – and also adding essential nutrients. In its most basic form it was done by opening a hatch from the river and allowing the water to run along the tops of ridges before trickling through the meadows and then returning to the river via specially dug drains. More complex were those that used a variety of sluices, hatches, drains, mains, carriers and channels.

In the 21st century, possibly the best places to see examples of existing water meadows are in Hampshire around Wherwell, Stockbridge and Fordingbridge; along the Wiltshire Avon and Nadder, and by the side of the Thames near Oxford – the last being cared for by the Hurst Water Meadow Trust.

From above, it is still just possible to see where the ditches integral to the flooding of grazing meadows used to run (the strips of darker grass running north to south of the photo).

DITCHERS AND DYKE-MEN

Elsewhere, ditches that simply carried surface water safely through farmland, into rivers and eventually out to sea were maintained either by the farmers themselves or by a travelling 'ditcher' who, in the same way as a hedge-layer, was paid by the distance to be dug or cleared. Farmers were often assisted by 'day-men' – casual workers who could turn their hand to anything, including ditch maintenance. One such worker who was around at the time when tractors were just beginning to take over from horses observed:

> Draining was all spadework then, and every wet spot had to be investigated. Tree roots, especially chestnut, were devils for blocking up the green lane. And in the open fields, we were forever replacing the [drain] tiles – in heavy ground they didn't want to be too deep and so they were always breaking because of the weight of the new machinery.

Various British government censuses taken between 1841 and 1911 also include the occupations of 'banker' (a person who dug ditches and trenches to allow drainage, placing surplus earth in banks alongside) and 'dyke-men' who variously tended to both ditches and hedges as the case arose. The old-fashioned council road-man who walked his beat and filled in pot-holes and repaired road edges was also responsible for ensuring that any ditches which ran alongside the public highway were kept free-running and clear of debris and that any subsidence was rectified.

THE MAN FOR THE JOB

Richard Jefferies, arguably the best and most descriptive country writer of all time, describes, in *Hodge and his Masters* (1880), the type of farm labourer likely to be responsible for hedge-trimming on the bank above a ditch:

Watch the man there – he slices off the tough thorns as though it were straw… Rain and tempest affect him not; the glaring heat of summer, the bitter frost of winter are alike to him. He is built up like an oak. Believe it, the man that from his boyhood has stood ankle-deep in the chill water of the ditch, patiently labouring with axe and bill; who has trudged across the furrow, hand on plough, facing sleet and mist; who has swung the sickle under the summer sun – this is the man for the trenches.

HOW DITCHES WERE BUILT

The road-men, bankers, ditchers, dyke-men and drowners had the benefit of knowledge gained from their predecessors. There has always been a basic set formulation when it comes to the construction of a ditch and even the ancient builders of war dykes worked on certain dimensions regarding height and base widths. Ure's *General View of the Agriculture in the County of Dumbarton* of the late 1700s tells us that the 'earth dyke is commonly four feet broad at the base, and from three to five feet high', while reprints of Primrose McConnell's 1883 *The Agricultural Handbook* have it that: 'Approximate dimensions depend mainly on the volume of water the ditch is expected to carry at peak flow times. This will depend on catchment area, soil type and gradient. Although formulae have been devised for calculating the required cross-sectional area of a ditch, most are constructed on a rule-of-thumb basis.' It goes on to further explain: 'The usual rule-of-thumb guide is to make the top width [of the bank] equal to the sum of the bottom width and the depth. On heavy clay land sides can be steeper than this but on lighter, sandy soils the batter [slope] should be about 30 degrees from horizontal.' More recently, John Seymour writing in *The New Complete Book of Self-Sufficiency* (2003) simply opined that: 'If you are having to dig the ditch by hand you won't want it too deep.'

TOOLS OF THE TRADE

At the very outset, digging ditches and dykes by hand was the only option. Our primary school history lessons pointed out that those likely to have been digging the first war dykes would have been equipped with not much more than rudimentary tools made from wood, flint and animal bone. Things improved during the Iron Age of course (the clue is in the name!) and eventually, blacksmiths forged and made both general digging implements as well as those specific for the purpose. A typical ditching spade would, for example, have had a shorter handle than one designed for all-round use due to the fact that its user would most likely be working in a confined space. For land drainage jobs, a plough might have been used to create a furrow. Originally pulled by oxen and later by horses, such things were subsequently done by steam engines.

The Industrial Revolution meant that major drainage works could be undertaken with relative ease by machinery (the various rural museums dotted about the country are good places to visit in order to find out more

– in particular, the Hollycombe Steam Collection at Liphook, Hampshire), and then all that was necessary was general maintenance and a periodic clear-out by hand in ensuing years.

The farming trends of the 1970s and '80s (the use of larger tractors and machinery and general economies of scale) meant that many smaller fields were amalgamated and the intervening ditches piped in and covered. In theory, with the aid of mole drainage cut at systematic parallels under the soil, this also had the merit of increasing the area of land available for cultivation and eliminated the labour costs involved with hedge and ditch maintenance. In practice, though, not all ditches were suitable for piping – particularly those which were acting as interceptors of surface water run-off. Eventually many pipes cracked and broke and areas which were once kept drained by ditches became water-logged again – none of which can have helped the flooding situations experienced by many in recent winters.

Latterly, more serious anti-flooding measures have been done by machine dredgers, and from Canada originates a most fearful-looking piece of kit known as a 'Wolverine' which, or so its makers claim:

> ... combines the features of a land scraper and utilizes the tractor's power take off to drive an upright steel rotating impeller, spreading the soil evenly on the field. This unique combination holds many benefits over existing systems: scraping and spreading are done in a single operation saving time and cost. Also the soil is spread evenly, for up to a 150-foot distance on either side of the ditch, facilitating the easy operation of today's large seeding, tillage, and harvesting equipment through and around the ditch.

DIGGING THE DEVIL'S DYKE

Of course, folklore and country custom would have it that some ditches or dykes were not man-made at all, but were the work of the Devil himself. Take, for instance, the theories connected with the creation of the Devil's Dyke in Sussex.

In one popular story, legend has it that, once the Christian church took hold and its teachings followed, the Devil became so agitated that

Not a 'Wolverine' but a pretty formidable-looking machine nonetheless. Things have come a long way since digging implements made from stag's antler were the only option!

he decided to dig a huge channel from the sea through the South Downs in order that the sea would then flood the surrounding countryside and drown all the inhabitants. Under the cover of darkness, he began digging at Poynings and had soon thrown up huge mounds of spoil from his excavations. However, so busy was he with his work, the Devil failed to notice that he'd been spotted by a wise old Sussex woman who, with commendable forethought, held a lit candle high behind a sieve and, with her other hand, pushed her sleeping cockerel from his perch. The Devil, hearing the indignant cock start crowing and seeing the light (which he mistook for the sun rising), fled the scene leaving his ditch half complete – and thus created the Devil's Dyke… and the piles of dug earth to become Chanctonbury and Cissbury Ring!

A DITCH IN TIME

The Devil makes work for idle hands they say but is it fair to assume that the ancients of Cambridgeshire and Sussex, for example, were any more indolent than the rest just because there are several Devil's Dykes dotted about the British countryside?!

In all but the most exceptional of circumstances, both excavations by the hand of the Devil as mentioned above – and by the use of machinery such as the 'Wolverine' mentioned before that – strike of over-kill in most of the situations likely to be found in Britain's countryside. There is, though, a very definite need to reinstate and/or maintain the ditches and dykes of old: not just for practical drainage and farming purposes, but also, most importantly, for the benefit of wildlife and conservation. Such practicalities are, though, best left until another chapter.

For now, neglected by many, understood by a few, those ditches that do survive today are a constant source of fascination and enjoyment throughout the year – particularly when it comes to their likely flora and fauna. With that in mind, is it not then surely time to look carefully at what one might expect to see if one is prepared to mooch and observe what goes on seasonally both in the ditch and on its banks? In fact, as the poet William Henry Davies famously wrote in *Leisure*, arguably his most noted work:

What is this life if, full of care,
We have no time to stand and stare.

No time to stand beneath the boughs
And stare as long as sheep or cows.

No time to see, when woods we pass,
Where squirrels hide their nuts in grass.

No time to see, in broad daylight,
Streams full of stars, like skies at night.

No time to turn at Beauty's glance,
And watch her feet, how they can dance.

No time to wait till her mouth can
Enrich that smile her eyes began.

A poor life this if, full of care,
We have no time to stand and stare.

'What is this life if, full of care, We have no time to stand and stare.'

2

EXPLORING A MODERN-DAY DITCH

In the *Just William* books written by Richmal Crompton, William Brown and his gang of 'Outlaws' can frequently be found poking about with sticks in ditches and, in one of her website blogs, Connie Smith (*http://grandmapearl.hubpages.com*) perfectly describes the similar activities of many country children over the decades. Although the latter is talking of a childhood in America, the fascination that youngsters have for water and what it might contain is universal:

> ... my brothers and I... put ourselves in charge of the ditch in front of our house. In the spring when things were beginning to thaw, we busied ourselves every day after school and on weekends. After finding a suitable 'ditch stick', we set about de-icing and pulling garbage from the ditch. If we found a clump of dead leaves and sticks clogging the flowing icy water that was placed on the upper edge out of the way. It was kind of a messy job, but that didn't matter to us!

Likewise, fellow American Sam Donaldson, journalist and famous news anchor-man, had this to say about his childhood:

> I was a typical farm boy. I liked the farm. I enjoyed the things that you do on a farm, go down to the drainage ditch and fish, and look at the crawfish and pick a little cotton.

Phil Rant, English poet and countryman, wrote the following as an explanatory prelude to one of his poems:

> An area I used to frequent in Scotland had many ditches, dykes and gullies which, during the

American children in the 1870s enjoying time at a ditch —
possibly engaged in a game of 'Poohsticks' before it became
known as such through the writings of A. A. Milne!

winter months were filled with running rain water
coming off the land above. As the rainfall eased in
the spring, these ditches still contained (by now,
stagnant) water and most summers they would
dry completely. Every spring I would note they
were full: first of frogspawn then later milliards of
tadpoles. I used to be concerned for their welfare;
surely as the ditches dried they would perish?

One year I came across some children from the
village a mile or so down in the valley below this
wild land. They had with them the ubiquitous
jam jars and showed me they had 'rescued' some
tadpoles to put in ponds down in the village.

I remember walking away with a sense that, whilst we may destroy much, and the numbers involved in the 'rescue' would make little difference, it was heart-warming that the new generation was learning.

Sadly, there is much in the current media about how today's children prefer to play computer games rather than participate in the kind of activities so enjoyed by their parents and grand-parents. Without the encouragement to climb trees, kick through autumn leaves, collect bugs and paddle about in ditches and streams, the psychologists worry that future generations will succumb to 'epidemic obesity, attention-deficit disorder, isolation and childhood depression'.

Richard Louv, in his book *Last Child in the Woods* (first published in 2005), refers to a phenomenon he calls 'nature deficit disorder' and claims that, as children spend less time outdoors, they are more prone to suffering from behavioural problems. Taking your children to mess about in a nearby ditch will help stop the rot!

WHAT TO WEAR

Even on the hottest of summer days, it's not a particularly good idea to go walking in a ditch bare-footed and dressed in naught but shorts and a tee-shirt. Shards of glass washed downstream and sharp stones exposed from the silt by winter rain do very little in the way of a pedicure. Some plants (such as giant hogweed)

TESTING THE WATER

Various conservation groups are always looking for volunteers to help with various monitoring projects in river, stream or ditch. As an example, the Arun & Rother Connections (West Sussex) Riverfly Project, launched in early 2016, asked for volunteers to carry out some 'kick samples' in the river bed and record the presence and numbers of eight invertebrate groups.

It's not just in obscure rural regions that volunteer water monitors are required either: the Thames Water for Wildlife is a 2016 survey aiming to build up a picture of water quality and nutrient pollution across their region. As they point out; 'Clean water is crucial to the wonderful wildlife that makes its home in freshwater. But whilst we know a lot about water quality in the River Thames and its major tributaries, the mosaic of thousands of ponds, lakes, ditches and streams in the Thames region remains largely unmonitored.

Children have long loved playing around ditches and streams – as this painting, Children by the Stream, by English artist Alexander Beydeman (1826–1869), shows.

can cause irritation or worse to exposed skin and some of the insects you've come to watch are capable of giving an unpleasant bite or sting on bare flesh. But don't let any of that put you off from spending time in a ditch – just be sure to wear the right attire.

The average countryside enthusiast is already likely to have an outdoor wardrobe suitable enough for mooching about in the ditch and the right sort of clothes can, depending on the time of year, undoubtedly make life more comfortable. There are, for instance, shirts, trousers, fleeces, jackets, socks and caps made to be tick-resistant, and these are of real value during the periods when ticks are likely to be active. Apparently endowed with tick-resistant protection during manufacture, the treatment is, according to the makers, 'odourless, skin-friendly, UV-proofed and machine washable'.

For winter wear, any coat or jacket needs to keep you dry and warm. A somewhat obvious statement perhaps, but the choice is as bewildering as it is useful. 'Gore-tex' and 'Teflon' treated coats and soft Loden jackets all help in keeping out the wind and rain and all breathable fabrics are brilliant in ensuring that you get neither too hot nor too cold, and work by wicking away moisture. A fleece, worn under a jacket on the coldest day, or a gilet in place of a jacket on the warmest, is also a useful addition to your wardrobe.

'VESTS AND PANTS AND BOOTS WITH LACES'

As a child, I used to love a comedy song sung to the tune of *Men of Harlech* – the lyrics for which were, I think, first written in the book *1066 and All That* (published in 1930) in which it was said that woad worn by the Ancient Britons was better than 'vests and pants and boots with laces...'. Woad, as useful though it may have been for some in frightening off the enemy, will not, however, adequately protect you from the vagaries of the British weather!

Whatever sort of shirt you choose, make sure that the cuffs do not protrude from those of your coat or jacket: wet cotton shirt cuffs can turn cold quickly on a wet day and create a chill throughout the wearer's body. Any 'under-layers' should be made of wool or some type of modern synthetic material that stays warm when wet, or repels moisture from the body. Like the wet cuffs of a shirt, moisture (whether it comes from the elements or as a result of perspiration) can turn cold very quickly during any period of inactivity. For this reason, I would suggest that polo necks such as those sold in shooting shops might solve the subject of shirt and under-layers in one fell swoop. For really cold days, thermal underwear is very definitely a worthwhile investment.

Boots ought to be tough enough to ward off thorns and be water-proof, at least on the bottom around the welt. Like any item of clothing, leather ankle boots take some time to wear in and feel really comfort-able. Once a pair of leather boots have been properly broken in, it pays to look after them in the hope that they will give years of protection and comfort. To that end, always remove the worst of the dirt and mud straight away and, if they are wet, stand them to dry out naturally in a warm airy place: don't, however, be tempted into placing them too close or even on top of a stove or radiator. Special bags of crystals that absorb moisture can be bought and these help to wick away the dampness from inside the boots. These bags must then be dried out before using them again. Failing that, the old traditional standby of using scrunched up newspapers stuffed inside boots certainly helps in absorbing wet resulting from walking through an over-deep ditch or similar stretch of water.

As far as Wellingtons are concerned, there are several manufacturers who specialise in creating quality, natural rubber boots perfect for the countryman and ditch-watcher. Long gone are the days of sloppy, ill-fitting farmer's boots and most by the likes of 'Le Chameau' or 'Aigle' incorporate a fitted design around the ankle and lower leg. Some are leather or Gore-tex lined for extra warmth and comfort – and may also have the added refinement of a full-length or part-length strong YKK zip down the side, which makes both getting into and out of them a great deal easier than it is with conventional Wellingtons.

There are nowadays plenty of alternatives to Wellingtons.

HATS AND GLOVES

In the countryside, the flat cap is traditional but its one disadvantage is that it does not keep your ears warm. A woolly hat will solve this problem and, unlike a trilby or any similar hat with a brim, is not likely to blow off when you're standing at the side of a ditch on a blustery winter's day.

As far as gloves are concerned, thin cotton ones are usually sufficient and keep your hands from being directly exposed to the cold air on dry

'CHECK, CLEAN, DRY'

Throughout this book – but particularly in the next chapter – there is plenty of evidence that many invasive non-native species can have a damaging impact on British plants, animals and ecosystems by spreading disease, competing for habitat and food, and direct predation. Plants that grow profusely can block waterways while some animals can damage riverbanks.

Not all invasive species are obvious to see and, as you dabble about in the ditch, you may be unwittingly helping to spread invasive species from one water body to another in equipment, shoes and clothing. The GB Non-Native Species Secretariat (NNSS) suggest taking the following precautions:

* Check your equipment and clothing for live organisms – particularly in areas that are damp or hard to inspect.
* Clean and wash all equipment, footwear and clothes thoroughly. Use hot water where possible.
* If you do come across any obvious organisms, leave them at the water body where you found them.
* Dry all equipment and clothing – some species can live for many days in moist conditions.

days. Leather shooting gloves are also good at such times and, if of a correct fit, should be like a second skin. They are not much good when it is raining, though, as they quickly get sodden and your hands very cold. When it's wet, fingerless wool or polypropylene gloves might be a better alternative. Best of all though, protect a pair of conventional gloves with a pair of surgical ones! If you buy them in as large a size as possible (they are cheap enough to buy by the box), surgical gloves can be worn over lightweight 'proper' gloves in the winter and make a big difference in keeping your hands clean and dry whilst exploring what a ditch might have to offer in the cold days of January.

THE WATER ELEMENT

Water is, of course, the main component of most ditches. Leonardo da Vinci wasn't wrong when he observed that 'water is the driving force of all nature'. Nor was Margaret Atwood, the Canadian poet, novelist and environmentalist, when she wrote: 'Water does not resist. Water flows… it goes where it wants to go, and nothing in the end can stand against it.'

Watercourses of all descriptions are, for many reasons, essential to many forms of wildlife, in particular in their provision of a vital food chain. Slow-running water – found in most ditches – is the ideal habitat for certain plants on which some invertebrates breed and feed; and both of these are, in turn, a part of the diet of many bird species. In unpolluted water, fish and amphibians live quite successfully and on the banksides, much grows to provide both a permanent and a temporary food source and home for insects, birds, water voles and larger mammals.

'Water flows… it goes where it wants to go, and nothing in the end can stand against it.'

'CHECK, CLEAN, DRY'

Throughout this book – but particularly in the next chapter – there is plenty of evidence that many invasive non-native species can have a damaging impact on British plants, animals and ecosystems by spreading disease, competing for habitat and food, and direct predation. Plants that grow profusely can block waterways while some animals can damage riverbanks.

Not all invasive species are obvious to see and, as you dabble about in the ditch, you may be unwittingly helping to spread invasive species from one water body to another in equipment, shoes and clothing. The GB Non-Native Species Secretariat (NNSS) suggest taking the following precautions:

  * Check your equipment and clothing for live organisms – particularly in areas that are damp or hard to inspect.
  * Clean and wash all equipment, footwear and clothes thoroughly. Use hot water where possible.
  * If you do come across any obvious organisms, leave them at the water body where you found them.
  * Dry all equipment and clothing – some species can live for many days in moist conditions.

WATER ANALYSIS

Whilst detailed water type analysis is way beyond the scope of a book of this generality, it is, however, worth making very brief mention of the fact that the water type of any given ditch is dependent on several things, the most obvious of which is that its alkalinity/acidity status is mainly determined by the surrounding soil structure. A predominantly chalk base is likely to result in alkaline water whereas a clay or woodland base will probably mean that the water in any nearby ditches is acidic.

Bogs, from which water may or may not drain into a ditch (and here it is important to remember that draining boggy land which is classified as a bog – particularly in a Site of Special Scientific Interest – may well be illegal), are generally characterised by wet, spongy, poorly drained peaty soil, dominated by the growth of bog mosses, and are usually acid areas (frequently surrounding a body of open water). According to those far better qualified than I to expound upon such subjects, bogs receive water almost exclusively as a result of rainfall.

Fenland is, on the other hand, a type of wetland ecosystem dominated by grasses, sedges and reeds and contains water that is alkaline rather than acid. Again according to the experts, fenland also differs by dint of the fact that the water contained therein is mainly derived from surface and groundwater sources (rather than by rainfall).

A commonality of all officially designated wetlands is that either the water table is very near to the soil surface or shallow water covers the surface for at least part of the year. The

KEEP IT CLEAN

The clarity and composition of the water running down any course intended to take it away from the land, and eventually to the sea, is worthy of consideration and although a ditch containing brackish water might not look very clean, colour is of less importance than the fact that it may contain herbicides and pesticides which have found their way there from the surrounding farmland. Interestingly, since the summer of 2014, the Environment Agency have been offering a 'real-time' service whereby one can monitor the clarity/pollution of water as it enters the sea via channels along the beach. It is still too early to come to any definitive conclusions, but it will be interesting to know the results of tests conducted in areas immediately around such freshwater outlets.

acid/alkaline content is, to some extent, determined by the combination of the salinity of the water in the wetland, the soil type and the plants and animals living there and thereabouts.

When it comes to the selection of Sites of Special Scientific Interest, freshwater habitats are divided into three groups: (a) standing waters (e.g. lakes, pools, ponds, gravel-pits, reservoirs and canals); (b) lowland ditch systems (e.g. in grazing marshes such as the water meadows described in Chapter 1) and finally, (c) flowing waters (rivers and streams). It was undoubtedly the last of which the poet John Clare wrote when he penned these two verses:

The green banks and the rustling sedge
I'll wander down at e'en
All sloping to the water's edge
And in the water green.

Could the poet John Clare have once met his 'lassie'
on this 'green bank... all sloping to the water's edge'?!

> And there's the luscious meadow sweet
> Beside the meadow drain
> My lassie there I once did meet
> Who I wish to meet again.

HEDGEROW HABITAT

In another of his poems, Clare perfectly describes the joy experienced by children released from school after a day of lessons – and how they often headed for the ditch or stream to do what youngsters have loved to do since time immemorial:

> Hark to that happy shout! —the school-house door
>   Is open thrown, and out the younkers teem;
> Some run to leap-frog on the rushy moor,
>   And others dabble in the shallow stream,
> Catching young fish, and turning pebbles o'er

For muscle shells. Look in that sunny gleam,
Where the retiring sun, that rests the while,
Streams through the broken hedge! How happy seem
Those friendly schoolboys leaning o'er the stile,
Both reading in one book! — Anon a dream,
Rich with new joys, doth their young hearts beguile,
And the book's pocketed right hastily.
Ah, happy boys! well may ye turn, and smile,
When joys are yours that never cost a sigh.

Note in particular the line where 'the retiring sun, that rests the while, Streams through the broken hedge!' Hedges are an important feature of the countryside and no more so than when planted at the top of a ditch bank where they form a practical purpose both as a field boundary and in that their roots hold together the bankside thus helping to prevent erosion.

A good hedge contains several species of native shrubs and trees and, at its bottom, a variety of vegetation and wild flowers. All of these are interesting in themselves, but importantly, they also play host to a myriad of tiny invertebrates, which in turn pollinate and/or provide a food source for larger insects and birds. Tragically, both hedges and ditches were grubbed out by the mile some 40 or so years ago in order to create larger fields for agricultural efficiency. Fortunately, however, many of these hedges are now being replaced, or new ones created, but not all have a ditch at their base – which is a great shame as far as ecology and wildlife is concerned. Add a ditch to the equation and such benefits are multiplied to a point almost beyond belief.

Snakeshead fritillaries are just one of many plants that thrive in a hedge bottom close to a ditch or small rural stream.

A VERSATILE TREE

In amongst the trees of a long-established hedgerow, it's often possible to see one of the several varieties of willow that

THE GREEN LIGHT DISTRICT

I am, and always have been, fascinated by glow worms which are, in fact, beetles and not worms at all. Small and otherwise insignificant (unless you happen to be another glow worm!), the quite bright, luminous green light they produce at night whilst tucked away in a hedgerow atop a ditch or dyke emits only from the female – and initially, is her way of advertising for a mate. Coming from such a tiny insect, the illumination emanating from the last few segments of her abdomen can be seen a surprising distance away – up to 50 metres/54 yards.

Unfortunately, being unequipped with Duracell batteries, the females only produce their glow for a few weeks (even after finding a mate and laying eggs, they continue giving off their light so as to deter predators), before dying.

In literature, Pliny referred to glow worms as 'glittering flies' whilst Wordsworth said they were 'earth-born stars'. Coleridge described a glow worm as a 'love torch'!

traditionally grow along a riverbank or at the edge of a watercourse. Some, indeed, might actually have their roots in the water and in doing so, play an important role in helping to keep the ditch-side structure intact.

If the hedge forms a boundary between field and water, there is a good chance that some of the older willows may have been pollarded by decades of farmers and other rural dwellers over the years. Pollarding is an ancient and well-known way of taking timber for a particular purpose whilst still allowing the tree to grow and thrive (think pruning in the orchard and garden) in order to be used again by future generations. Some trees were pollarded to simply provide logs for a winter fire but the willow was far more versatile than that and was, therefore, often encouraged and maintained. Likely uses include – depending on the variety – logs, fencing stakes, boarding (and brake blocks) for farm carts, shingle tiles for the shed roof (although sweet chestnut was the preferred choice when available), wood for charcoal (but again, chestnut or even hazel was the wood of choice in certain regions), young growth for weaving into baskets and, of course, the making of cricket bats.

It depends which part of the British Isles you find yourself in, but probably the most commonly noticed type is the crack willow. This is easily identifiable by its rough, coarse bark and its brittle branches – try snapping a smallish piece by bending it upwards.

Identifying other trees, vegetation, birds and animals likely to be discovered along the length of a ditch might not, however, be quite so simple and there might need to be a certain degree of detective work involved.

PLAYING DETECTIVE

Provided that you've no holes in your boots and plenty of time on your hands, there are few things more pleasurable than paddling about in an interesting ditch, no matter whether you are one of the children mentioned in John Clare's poem above, or are of a slightly more mature generation!

The young growth of willow has been used for weaving baskets for many centuries. (Photo: courtesy of Nick Hinchliffe)

One of the great things about ditches is that there are, at most times of the year, usually odd muddy patches to be found somewhere along their length – and these are wonderful places to play 'nature detective'. Any clear damp area will often show the footprints of birds and animals and it is surprising just how much evidence of different species one can glean, even though you might rarely see the bird or beast that created them.

FOOT-FOLLOWERS

Look out for any worn crossing points as it is quite likely they are made by deer or hares, the prints of which can often be easily seen. With experience, it is even possible to work out the individual deer species: roe have smaller, more closed hoof prints than do, say, fallow deer. Evidence of webbed feet will suggest wild duck – most likely mallard – and sprawled-out bird prints with just a touch of 'webbing' between them, either coots or moorhens. Pheasants like marshy areas (they are, in their original form, most naturally a bird of the marshes despite the fact that they are now most likely to be seen on farmland and at woodland edges) and their chicken-like footprints are easy to spot. As otters are now known to frequent every county, it might even be possible to see their footprints in the mud. However, it is probably more likely that they were made by mink. The mink's pad-marks are smaller than otters' but, unless you have the two to compare, how can you tell?! Notes, sketches and photographs will help in any 'identification parade' once you get home and have access to both the internet and any reference books.

Now you see me, now you don't

Mink have undoubtedly had a detrimental effect on water vole numbers and have been officially cited as one of the major contributing factors in that species' on-going demise. Thankfully, though, as a result of tremendous efforts on the part of water authorities and others, the vole is making a steady comeback (see *Water voles* in the following chapter). In places they do frequent, they are not always the easiest animals to observe. Despite keeping totally still on the ditch bank and carefully watching the water, it is still possible that one could easily pass close by without you being aware of its presence – the reason being that they have flaps of skin over their ears to keep the water out and, because of this particular evolutionary refinement, are able to swim by you almost totally submersed. Even if you don't see the animals themselves, during the summer months you might be made aware of their presence by small clues such as vertical shafts which open up near the water's edge and around which the vegetation might well be cropped close as a result of the voles feeding close-by.

ARTIFICIAL BUT STILL INDICATIVE

The ditch detective should bear in mind the fact that such waterways are, in the main, man-made and are, therefore, something of an artificial environment. While there are many plants and grasses to discover, their presence is not necessarily indicative of the naturally occurring true aquatic vegetation of the region in the present day – but (unless intentionally introduced by man or accidentally by wildlife) they do offer some clues as to what once might have grown there before meadows and marshes were drained. Biologists are of the opinion that plants such as marsh marigolds, watercress, gypsywort, flag irises and reeds were originally swamp-loving plants rather than frequenters of actual watercourses.

Areas of mud along the ditch are the perfect places
to look for signs of animal and bird tracks.

THE ROOT OF THE MATTER

Whilst you are far less likely than a water vole to be able to identify the nutritional goodness or otherwise of certain types of vegetation, it is possible to recognise whether a particular plant or grass is an annual, biennial or perennial by looking at its roots. Look for rhizomes, bulbs, tubers or large, fleshy roots, all of which are usually indicative of perennials (whilst at the same time bearing in mind the fact that young perennials are sometimes difficult to tell apart from annuals because they have not yet developed these structures). Rhizomes and similar root growth swell with maturity and are used to store and provide winter feed, allowing new stems to emerge in the spring.

Germination time is another point of consideration when it comes to identifying vegetation found in a ditch. Summer annuals almost always germinate in spring or early summer whereas winter annuals (and many biennials) germinate in late summer or autumn. Conversely, perennials can germinate at almost any period (but do so predominantly in spring and autumn). Knowing all this makes it far easier to look up the relevant section in a plant identification book and find out both the common and Latin name of an individual grass or plant type.

Some plants are so similar it is easy to confuse them, particularly when the likes of garden escapees such as Star of Bethlehem can be found growing wild in places also frequented by wild garlic – the flowers of which look very similar. Both also have bulbous roots.

CLEAN AIR ACT

A dyke (accepting the definition as explained in Chapter 1, i.e. an earth bank with a ditch at its base and either a wall or hedge at its top) can offer many clues to the nature detective. Lichen growing on a wall or the branches of a hedgerow helps assess the purity of the atmosphere (the more there is to see, the cleaner the air) and, in some instances, even indicate a compass direction. If there is an abundance of lichen on one side of the hedge or tree, and little or none on the other, it's a reasonably safe bet to assume that where moss appears is facing south or slightly south-west – from which you can get your bearings.

TAKING NOTE

As mentioned above, in true detective style, you should take notes at the 'scene of the crime'. A small, fairly robust notebook is always worth keeping to hand and, to my mind, a *Moleskine*® is the answer (for a countryperson, it's an appropriate name too!). Whilst it might not be totally waterproof, its hardback cover is of a kind that will withstand a lot of abuse and its pages are of good enough quality to be able to cope with hands that might, at times, be less than clean. I take a diary-sized one with me to make notes when out and about as it slips in any pocket quite easily, but there are other sizes available.

A camera is also useful in collecting 'evidence'. As most mobile phones these days have a camera facility, it could be argued that a separate camera might be an unwarranted encumbrance but, generally speaking, a camera will undoubtedly produce better results than anything taken via a phone.

BEATING TRAYS AND POOTERS

It is all very well to know that there are likely to be plentiful invertebrates, bugs and insects sequestered in the long grasses and other vegetation that can be found on the side of a ditch, but getting to see them is another matter entirely. Using a 'beating tray' in the spring and summer is certainly one way of seeing what's going on.

On their website, the Amateur Entomologists' Society (*www.amentsoc.org*) explains that a beating tray generally consists of a pale-coloured cloth stretched out over a frame. The frame is then held under a likely place for specimens and the foliage gently shaken. Invertebrates, bugs and beetles fall from the foliage and land on the cloth – from where they can then be examined or collected using a 'pooter'. As few uninvolved with bug-collecting are likely to know what the latter piece of equipment is, the Society's website very usefully enlightens the reader with the following information:

A pooter consists of a collection vessel (often a plastic or glass jar) with a tight fitting lid. The lid has two holes in it and a tube inserted into each hole. One tube has a fine mesh over the end inside the jar.

The entomologist sucks on the open end of the tube that has the mesh at the other end. At the same time the end of the second tube is aimed at an invertebrate. The suction draws the invertebrate down the second tube and into the collection vessel. The fine mesh on one tube prevents the entomologist swallowing any invertebrates.

A STEALTHY APPROACH

Admittedly, mooching along the banks of your nearest ditch is not in any way akin to exploring the Amazon or going on an African safari but, nevertheless, a stealthy approach least disturbs wildlife. Whilst the insects will take little notice of your arrival (and will, indeed, be grateful of it if they are the kind to bite and feed from your blood or sweat!) and most songbird species return in a very short space of time if, once you are at your chosen observation point, you remain still and quiet, others will not be so forgiving of your intrusion. Previously resting mammals will be gone for the duration and your clumsy arrival might well be sufficient to frighten a sitting waterbird away from its nest on the bankside.

Whilst a walk in the countryside without a dog is considered incomplete by many, should you decide to take your beloved pooch along, take care that he or she doesn't disturb any nests or dig at holes which may be home to small mammals such as water voles. A paddling dog is also likely to churn up the bed of the ditch and, quite literally, muddy the water – making any observation difficult until all has settled once more. J. E. Marriat-Ferguson, writing in his book *Visiting Home* (1905), recounted an intended ditch-dipping expedition with his godson James:

> I'd not long been back at Audley Hall when the opportunity arose to educate The Boy into the countryside's springtime resurgence. Planning our walk carefully, we came by Grove Wood ... and then to the ditch which fed the Lake. It was my intention to show him much in the way of frog spawn; the vole holes I remembered vividly from my youth... and possibly even catch sticklebacks (for which we'd come well equipped with jar and nets). I'd not, however, anticipated the extra company from James's dogs which he insisted joined us on our journey.
>
> Dauntless, the foxhound puppy (being walked by the family for the local hunt), was here, there, and everywhere and, despite continual admonishment, was determined to do as he would. So too was James's pair of terriers, Pippin and Grip. Together,

A stealthy approach least disturbs wildlife – and brings unexpected rewards. This damselfly was seen eating the wings and carcass of another. Whilst cannibalism is not uncommon in both damselflies and dragonflies, is this one eating the remains of a mate or simply an opportunist feeding on a damselfly found trapped in the spider's web?

the trio were as efficient as a pack of otterhounds in clearing the ditch banks of any form of wildlife either avian or four-legged. When we got to the water, all three were in with a splash and there was no choice but to change the intended nature walk into nothing more than hound exercise.

3

FASCINATING FLORA AND FAUNA

Ditches and their surroundings are the ideal habitat for much flora and fauna. In fact, it is reckoned that nearly half of the aquatic plant species of Britain can be found in small streams and ditches (as opposed to large rivers, ponds and lakes). Birds and animals use the bankside vegetation for nesting, resting and as a food source, and the damp conditions created by a ditch or similar water passage, plus overhanging tree branches and the like, make the perfect home and breeding grounds for many types of insects. Crickets, grasshoppers, butterflies, moths and the rapidly vanishing bumblebee can often also be found in this perfect environment.

Rarely does nature work in isolation. Take, for instance, this example. Many insects have aquatic larval stages and bats take advantage of the emerging insects. Bats need open water to drink, and bankside vegetation provides food and valuable cover for foraging. Some species preferentially select roost sites close to water. Importantly, threats to some species of bats arise as a result of habitat changes – including habitats generally described as riparian, wetland, woodland and unimproved grassland – which have affected hitherto insect-rich feeding areas. In addition, the loss and decline of linear landscape features (e.g. tree lines, hedgerows and ditches) remove important flyways and flight-line features along which bats hunt for insect prey.

INSECTS

CRICKETS AND GRASSHOPPERS

Both crickets and grasshoppers love long uncut grass – no wonder they can often be heard along the fringe where the bank of a ditch borders onto a farmer's field. More commonly heard than seen, if you sit quietly it is, however, possible observe them – and maybe even see exactly how they produce the noise they do (an important part of both a mating ritual and a way of proclaiming their territory). Interestingly, the cricket makes its

The grasshopper makes its distinctive sound by rubbing its back legs against its wings. (Photo: Alvesgaspar/ Wikimedia Commons)

distinctive sound by rubbing its wings together, whereas the grasshopper uses its back legs to rub against its wings. If you are able to watch them, the cricket is the larger of the two – but then again, such information is probably useless unless you have the two more or less side by side in order to compare!

BUTTERFLIES AND MOTHS

Not all butterflies are butterflies – some are daytime-flying moths! Although it is generally assumed that moths are somewhat bland and boring in colour and only fly and feed at night, there are in fact several that are quite colourful and go about their business during daylight hours. Whilst the preferred habitat of both butterflies and moths can vary from upland to downland, woodland to mountain, there are some that are most likely to be found in the wet or damp places that ditches so admirably provide. The English subspecies of the swallowtail butterfly, for example, is, according to *Butterflies & Moths of Britain and Europe*, 'restricted to wet fenland', whilst the large heath is 'a butterfly of wet moorlands but also occurs in lowland marshes and bogs'. Some moths – the common wainscot, for instance – are particularly associated with wet areas in general whilst others, like the chimney sweeper, specifically frequent damp ditches. For some, a wet environment is crucial: according to David Carter, author of *Butterflies & Moths of Britain and Europe*, 'The caterpillars of the brown china-mark moth feed on pondweeds and are semi-aquatic'.

Some butterflies and moths depend entirely on the vegetation to be found by ditches and other damp places.

BUMBLEBEES

Wild spring flowers of many types are essential for the queen bumblebee as she wakes up from a winter of hibernation and looks for food in order to gain much-needed energy for the breeding period ahead.

Not for nothing did the saying 'as busy as a bee' come about: once her energy levels are restored, the queen will search out a nest site which, on the ditch bank, could be a (disused) mouse hole in the ground, or in tussocky grass. Laying down a larder of suitable nectar and pollen, she lays her first batch of eggs, and the emerging larvae eat their way through her carefully provided store before then pupating into adult worker bees. Workers by name, and certainly by nature, their duties are to provide more pollen and nectar for the further offspring of the queen – who will by now be laying eggs again.

The bees that hatch off towards the end of summer and into early autumn cease to be workers and are instead breeding males and young queens produced exclusively to be the patriarchs and matriarchs of next year's bee stocks. Once having mated with young bees from other nests (bumblebees tend not to 'colonise', unlike their honeybee cousins) so as to prevent in-breeding, the males, workers and original queen bee all die off – leaving just the new queens to hibernate in preparation for the whole complicated cycle to begin again the following spring.

MAYFLIES AND 'SEDGE-FLIES'

Mayflies – the fisherman's friend! On some of the most prestigious trout rivers of Britain, the seasonal mayfly hatch will have most fishing purists rushing for their rods, reels and tackle, such is the excitement engendered. There are, though, more than one type but in all, the adult stage is short-lived. The nymphs live out their particular stage of the mayfly cycle buried in the river or ditch bottom before typically emerging as an adult around the time of year from which they derive their name. Trout are fond of feeding on emerging mayflies and the fly boxes of most trout fishermen contain a plethora of imitation mayflies and their nymphs!

Whilst you might find trout fishermen who refer to 'sedge-flies', the naturalist is more likely to call them caddis flies and explain that their alternative moniker comes from the tendency of the adult caddis fly to attach themselves to the sedge grass growing along the banks of the water. Their size varies, but the main common characteristics of the 'sedge' are its wings and colour. An adult has two pairs of wings (a slightly longer set at the front and a shorter set at the rear). It also has long antennas which extend from the body, while the body itself tends to be of muted colours such as grey, brown, orange or green in order to help protect from predators (such as trout!). Caddis tend to hatch either early or late evening, which is undoubtedly the best time to see them.

Yellow mayfly. (Photo: Michael Palmer/ Wikimedia Commons)

ONCE BITTEN...

When it comes to insects, irrespective of whether or not you are equipped with a beating tray and pooter as described in the previous chapter, you will, before very long, discover some fascinating and often colourful specimens. In fact, one of the very few disadvantages of spending time in a ditch, particularly during the summer months, is that they will discover you – as a result of which you are quite likely to return homeward-bound complete with an enviable collection of insect and midge bites. It is, incidentally, only the females of midges which bite... not that that little snippet of information is likely to make any difference at all to the irritation and unpleasantness once bitten! When contemplating any serious ditch-exploration, it might then pay to arm yourself with insect repellent and/or a tube of cream suitable for soothing bites. If you know you are allergic to wasp stings and similar, a few antihistamine tablets are also a good idea.

Mosquitoes and midges

No-one likes a mosquito, particularly in the bedroom as it buzzes round your head on a summer's evening just when you are dropping off to sleep! Even more unpopular are midges. Midge problems are nothing new to the countryside-lover. Writing in 1860, fisherman Charles Weld remarked:

> Talk of solitude! ... why, every square yard contains a population of millions of these little harpies that pump blood out of you with amazing savageness and insatiability. Where they come from is a puzzle. While you are in motion not one is visible, but when you stop a mist seems to curl about your feet and legs, rising, and at the same time expanding, until you become painfully sensible that the appearance is due to a cloud of gnats. When seven miles from Scourie I came to the Laxford, a glorious salmon river spanned by a bridge... I had no longer sat down than up rose millions of midges, which sent me... half mad.

Both mosquitoes and midges are likely to be found around stagnant rather than flowing water and so a well-maintained, free-flowing ditch should not encourage their numbers. Because of recent flooding, though, it seems their numbers are increasing due to the fact that ditch and river overfill has left isolated patches of water which eventually becomes stagnant and so provides the perfect breeding ground for midges. Conversely (and very sadly), the nation's numbers of damselflies and dragonflies are not faring anywhere near so well.

DAMSELFLIES AND DRAGONFLIES

Is there any better way to enjoy being by a water's edge than having the additional accompaniment of damselflies and dragonflies? They are, as much as the first hearing of a cuckoo or the lazy cooing of turtle doves, a very definite indicator of summer. However, like the cuckoo and turtle dove, both damselfly and dragonfly numbers (particularly dragonflies) are declining in some parts of Britain – due in no small part to the flooding of ditches in recent years. It's not generally known that the damsel and dragonflies we see on a summer's day whilst out mooching fly only for anywhere between one and three weeks and yet, from creation to death, may spend inordinately longer actually in water.

In April 2014, the Canal and River Trust launched a project encouraging people to advise them of not only dragonflies but also other insects and wildlife seen on the water and on the banksides – the reason being that 'fluctuating river levels and fast currents can wash away dragonfly larvae, known as nymphs, and as the larvae live underwater for up to three years, the floods could have a long-term effect on dragonfly populations'.

Somewhat ironically, an increase in mosquito and midge numbers (upon which dragonflies avidly feed) brought by flooding ought to have benefited the immediate food chain and helped the survival of damsel and dragonflies – were it not for the fact that many of their nymphs had been washed from ditches during the winter months and, left exposed on banksides or across flooded fields, proved easy prey for birds and small mammals.

WATER-BEETLES AND BOATMEN

Even the smallest garden pond made from not much more than an upturned dustbin lid has the potential to provide a home for water-beetles, water-boatmen and certain types of water-snails so it would be rare to find a ditch that doesn't offer the ideal habitat for these and many

Dragonflies are declining in some parts of Britain, due in no small part to the flooding of ditches in recent years. (Photo: courtesy of Helen Tait-Wright)

more. Generally, the likes of the whirligig beetle and pond-skaters live on the water surface, as do both greater and lesser water-boatmen. The former type is sometimes called the 'backswimmer' because it swims upside-down in order to catch creatures that fall onto the surface of the pond, whilst the latter feeds mainly on plants and swims as one might expect. Water-boatmen are easily identified because of the 'sculling' action of their strong swimming 'oars' on each side of their body.

Both the water stick-insect and water scorpion usually live in the mud in shallow water but will, periodically, send up their hollow straw-like tail to the surface in order that they can breathe.

VEGETATION

To be successful, any kind of insect does, of course, require a near-perfect habitat, much of which is comprised of flowers, grasses and other incidental vegetation to be found within a ditch environment. Grasses help reduce soil erosion, and many types have developed in such a way that they are perfectly adaptable to the fluctuations in moisture conditions brought about by the alternating seasonal extremes between winter and summer. Depending on their type, they can make excellent nesting and/or 'escape' cover for many varieties of birds, and their seeds will even provide them with a useful source of feed.

Much of what you might find growing in a ditch depends on the locality: some plants will only grow in the warmer parts of Britain while others, such as the bog pimpernel, will most com-

ANIMAL, VEGETABLE OR MINERAL?
Quite often, as one stares intently, eyes down, into a ditch, it is possible to become convinced that the bubbles emanating from the muddy bottom are an indicator of something living. So they might but, more often, the bubbles are a result of a chemical reaction caused by the gaseous decomposition of organic matter which has fallen into the ditch over several months or even years. Its main properties are methane – and it is known by some as 'marsh gas'.

monly only be found by the side of upland ditches in the north. Marsh mallow is generally seen in ditches close to the sea but will occasionally appear by the side of those further inland.

There are some very attractive flower species inhabiting ditches and similar waterways: amongst them are common skullcap, purple loosestrife, sneezewort, various marsh orchids, viper's bugloss, water figwort, water pepper and water mint. Rare, and only appearing in British ditches as a result of it 'escaping' from a garden environment, is New Zealand willow-herb which, unlike its native cousin that stands a metre or so in height, is only a few centimetres tall. Whereas the native willow-herb can be found growing in poor, dry soil, the New Zealand variety particularly loves damp ditches along the roadside.

It is oft-quoted that 'a weed is just a flower growing in the wrong place' but I prefer to think of the lines written by the poet William Henry Davies during his later years:

Now I grow old, and flowers are my weeds,
I think of days when weeds were flowers;
When Jenny lived across the way,
And shared with me her childhood hours…

Some garden plants 'escape' – and find the conditions afforded by a ditch bank ideal.

FERNS

Ferns are quite fascinating plants and there's certainly far more to them than first meets the eye! One of the oldest plant varieties, their fossilised leaves are frequently found and are a reminder of prehistoric times. In fact the name of the UK's most eminent and knowledgeable groups on the subject (with no less a person than HRH the Prince of Wales as its patron) leads one to think of such an era of history.

The British Pteridological Society (BPS) actually takes its name from the Latin *Pteridophytes*, a collective name for over 75 species of British ferns, some of which thrive in moorland areas (bracken is an example) whilst others prefer the environment of cliffs, walls, woodland and ground cover. The varieties of most interest to the ditch explorer are, though, those that live in damp ground. These are some of the rarest and include the royal, marsh and hard fern.

Their preferred growing medium is a moist, yet not waterlogged, soil that has a pH level slightly on the acid side of 7 – and, according to the BPS, on 'sloping sites where the ground water is not static'. Ditches and similar water sources must, then, provide almost perfect conditions for wild, native ferns, and sympathetically managed ones are one of the best ways of ensuring the survival of some of the UK's less commonly seen examples.

Ditches and similar water sources provide perfect conditions for many of our native ferns, some of which remain evident even in the middle of winter.

BIRDS, BEASTS AND FISHES

It is actually very unlikely that a drainage ditch of the type under discussion will play host to many types of fish. Most are more at home in streams and rivers but there is always the possibility of discovering the likes of sticklebacks which have found their way there from the streams into which a ditch will eventually run. In the spring there might, though, be a glimpse of what at first might be thought to be 'shoals' of tiny fish in the water but which will, upon closer inspection, turn out to be tadpoles!

TOADS, FROGS AND NEWTS

Contrary to popular opinion, although both the common and natterjack (the latter nowadays being quite rare) toad need water in which to mate and breed, they spend most of their year on land – and sometimes quite dry land at that. In the spring, though, the environs of a ditch could well prove to be an ideal habitat. It is not unusual for toads and frogs to share the same ponds and waterways during this time but most naturalists agree that the common toad spawns later than the common frog.

Frog spawn can appear as early as the New Year in a mild winter although cold, heavy weather may delay its appearance until spring: it is, though, quite tough stuff and capable of surviving all but the harshest of cold spells – even if laid very early on in the year. The most likely type of frog to be observed is the common type which, as its name suggests, is widespread throughout Britain. Similar to the common variety is the marsh frog which was introduced into the marshes of Kent in 1935.

Newts are fascinating! In the spring the males appear more brightly coloured than at any other times of the year and they also develop a crest along the back and down the tail. On the great-crested newt (the largest of British newts), the crest becomes jagged and resembles the teeth of a saw blade. The male palmate newt grows a filament, like a fine black wire, from the tip of its tail – and its hind feet become webbed. The smooth newt female is similar to the female palmate but can, nevertheless, be identified by its spotted throat.

In his 1906 children's book, *Pond and Stream*, author Arthur Ransome recounts a somewhat sexist fairy story as to how the male newts got their crest:

Once upon a time there were two brown newts who lived in a pond. One was a he, and the other was a she, and neither of them knew which was which, or who ought to obey orders. So they swam about, and presently poked their noses up through the water-weed, and explained their difficulty to a gay old kingfisher, who was sitting in his rainbow cloak on a bough that hung over the water. They both asked the question at once. Only one of them asked about a dozen times, and went on asking, and the other asked just once very angrily, and then said nothing more. So the kingfisher, who was clever, knew which was which. 'Why, you are the he,' said the kingfisher to the angry one, and he took a brilliant feather from his breast and gently stroked the newt from his head to his tail. And then a queer thing happened. A fiery crest appeared all along its back, and its body became emerald and spotted gold; and the little she-newt clapped her hands to see her handsome husband, and now she always does exactly what he tells her.

It's not much of a ditch that doesn't provide the perfect environment for a frog! (Photo: courtesy of Helen Tait-Wright)

SNAILS

It's possible to find slugs and snails in and around the damp edges of a ditch but, hopefully, no puppy dog's tails as in the children's nursery rhyme!

Many varieties of water snails live in a ditch containing relatively pure water and for some of them, occasional flooding is not always a bad thing. Floods can prove vital in the re-colonisation of some types of water snails – especially the ramshorn whirlpool snail which inhabits ditches running through low-lying fields most likely to flood. As the ditch over-tops, snails are washed into the fields and eventually carried to other ditches – provided, that is, they don't become stranded as the water recedes and fall foul to predation by birds.

FRESHWATER LEECHES

Leeches are often found in a ditch – not that many people bother to look for them these days now that chemists no longer need to stock them and doctors are less inclined to attach them to their patients! A century or so ago they were, though, in great demand and not only by the medical profession as they did, apparently, make very effective weather barometers, as witnessed by this particular entry in the early Victorian encyclopaedia *Enquire Within*. After placing a leech in a jar filled with water (changing the latter once a week in summer and once a fortnight in winter) and covering the top of the jar with muslin, it was possible to gauge the weather by the following observations:

If the weather is to be fine, the leech lies motionless in the bottom of the glass; if rain may be expected, it will creep up to the top of its lodgings and remain there till the weather is settled; if we are to have wind, it will move through its habitation with amazing swiftness, and seldom goes to rest till it begins to blow hard. If heavy storms are to be expected, it will lodge for some days before, almost continually out of the water, and discover great uneasiness in violent throes and convulsive motions; in frost as in clear summer weather it lies constantly at the bottom; and in snow as in rainy weather it pitches its dwelling at the very mouth of the phial.

EELS

There are many animals and birds whose navigating and homing instinct can only ever be wondered at, but, as amazing as it is that a swallow, for instance, should migrate and then return via thousands of miles to the place where it was hatched, for me the amazing lifestyle of the eel takes some beating. It travels miles and ranges through many waterway systems before heading seawards and to traditional spawning grounds but, during its freshwater stages, it's just as likely to be found in a sluggish, brackish ditch as it is in the purest chalk stream.

Able to take on a colour most suited to the type of environment found at the bottom of its chosen stream or ditch, the European eel can appear brown or yellow. They can also survive just as well in relatively polluted water as they can in the gin-clear chalk stream. Their diet is eclectic: the rotting carcass of a drowned and undiscovered sheep is as welcome as the naturally occurring invertebrates, insect larvae, worms and occasional mollusc. Small fish and frogs might also appear on the menu.

From all that, one could assume that the eel is a gluttonous beast but, just to add to its mystery, it eats little if anything during the winter and prefers instead to hide inactively away in any conveniently occurring holes – possibly in a state of semi-hibernation: even in today's scientific world, not all is known about their lifestyle and some believe that eels may feed as snakes do and slowly digest a meal until their stomachs are completely empty.

LAMPREYS

I do not remember all that much from my schoolboy history lessons, but one thing that has, for some reason, always stuck in my mind is the fact that King Henry I (1068–1135) was supposed to have died as a result of eating a 'surfeit of lampreys'! Quite which type was the downfall of this particular monarch I'm not sure; however, in Britain today, there are three varieties that live in fresh water.

The brook lamprey is the smallest and most likely to be seen (although none are common, it is the commonest) but all are quite primitive in having no lower jaws and a mouth surrounded by a round sucker containing rasping teeth. Sometimes called 'stone-suckers' because of their habit of moving stones with their mouths in order to make a nest for spawning in the spring, brook lampreys spend much of their lifespan in places such as ditches where they can easily burrow in the mud and silt at the water's bottom.

Like eels, lampreys are fascinating, somewhat mysterious creatures. However, it is known that the (blind) larvae live as such for as long as six years before metamorphosis into adults, when they breed and spawn after which time they die – a little like the ill-fated King Henry!

SNAKES

Is it an eel, a lamprey – or a snake?! If, during a foray in your local ditch, you happen to see something slither down the bank and take to the water in order to escape possible threat, it is most likely to be a grass snake as, unlike the adder and the rare, endangered smooth snake which generally prefer drier conditions, they are quite at home in water. They are harmless to humans but perhaps not quite so much to the likes of frogs, their tadpoles and small fish, all of which form a part of their regular diet.

BIRDS

Often easier to hear than they are to see, you don't have to spend long on a stretch of ditch before encountering one type of songbird or another. Some will be found almost anywhere but many others favour a specific waterside environment – one of the major reasons being that there's a rich and ready source of protein in the form of insects and invertebrates. Wider ditches with plenty of reedy growth at their edges might prove to be the ideal habitat for such bird species as bearded tits, reed buntings and both sedge and reed warblers, whilst almost anywhere remotely water-filled is likely to be home to a family of moorhens.

Moorhens have, despite their moniker, nothing whatsoever to do with the upland moors and it is most likely their name is a corruption of the word 'mere', meaning a watery place. They are smaller than the similar-shaped coot and the two can most easily be differentiated by the fact that the moorhen has red colouring on the forehead whilst the coot has a somewhat larger, white-coloured forehead and what, in a chicken, would be its comb.

Above: Coots and moorhens are easy to differentiate: the moorhen has red colouring on the forehead... (Photo: courtesy of Helen Tait-Wright)

Left: ...whilst the coot has a somewhat larger, white-coloured forehead. (Photo: courtesy of Kirsteen Atkinson)

An enclosed ditch is not necessarily going to be attractive to the gloriously iridescent-coloured kingfisher. Firstly, there are not usually the fish stocks in a ditch that there are in a wider stream or river and secondly, kingfishers like to fly and hunt along more open stretches of water. Almost always, a kingfisher will dive into the water from a convenient fence post or tree stump – but will occasionally 'hover' before it dashes into the water to catch a fish. Once caught, its prey is stunned by being beaten on a convenient branch or post before being eaten head-first.

A kingfisher generally prefers to dive into the water from a convenient fence post or tree stump. (Photo: J. M. Garg/ Wikimedia Commons)

Many birds can be affected by long periods of flooding. Perhaps most obviously, sudden unusually high water levels may flood a kingfisher's nest situated in a bankside hole. Less obvious is the fact that when water lays on top of what should be relatively dry land for any period of time, many of the worms and insects that form an important part of a certain bird species' diet are drowned.

FOREIGN... BUT BECOMING NATURALISED

The little egret (the 'great' is the size and shape of a heron and, as yet, is rarely seen in Britain) was first noticed in the late 1980s – it first bred in Dorset – since when numbers have increased and the population spread throughout the south and into East Anglia. Whilst it is, it must be admitted, mainly seen in coastal areas (where there is both a resident and migratory population), it is becoming increasingly common to encounter them inland and I've frequently seen them in tributary ditches to streams and rivers on the Hampshire/Dorset border. There is, then, always a possibility that ditch-watchers in certain areas of the UK could quite easily catch a glimpse of a little egret – particularly in the autumn and winter when their numbers temporarily increase due to the arrival of migrants from the continent.

BEASTS

As you wander down a ditch, a fox might occasionally be disturbed. The vegetation and a sheltered spot make the banks of such places the perfect resting and sunning spot during the daytime. As indeed it does for many mammals, the ditch also provides a useful and relatively safe passageway for foxes to move through their hunting territory totally undisturbed and unseen.

Hedgehogs

Hedgehogs love a ditch, especially one located at the bottom of a hedgerow as there are all the components necessary to provide it with a perfect habitat. The hedge itself offers daytime shelter and, when the winter comes, a warm relatively sheltered place in which to hibernate amongst all of autumn's dead leaves. The banks and immediate environs of a ditch are good food sources as they are generally well stocked with the types of insects, worms, caterpillars, slugs and snails so beloved by hedgehogs. Being omnivorous creatures, they will eat the occasional young songbird chick fallen from its nest; or even carrion from larger birds and animals which have died in the ditch, or have been pulled there by larger predators such as foxes.

Hedgehogs have a far-reaching night-time hunting range in search of food (up to four kilometres or so) and a long length of ditch line most definitely facilitates their search. Too steep-sided a ditch is not, though, good news for them as they can get stuck at its base and then be unable to scramble back out to safety.

Water voles

'Ratty', the hero of Kenneth Grahame's book *The Wind in the Willows*, was not a rat at all, but was in fact a water vole. Sadly, water voles have, until relatively recently, been one of the most endangered mammal species in the UK and it was reckoned that their numbers had dropped by an alarming 94 per cent during the final 50 years of the last century. During the last decade and a half, though, thanks to the sterling efforts of various river authorities and conservation volunteers, numbers have increased substantially and, although their distribution is patchy in places, they can be found throughout England, Wales and Scotland.

Somewhat bizarrely, flooding may, in some circumstances, have a beneficial effect in that it allows numbers to re-distribute and re-colonise

The steep sides of some ditches can be a literal death-trap for hedgehogs.

(see also page 127). However, it can unfortunately have a negative effect by encouraging flood survivors to seek an alternative, and sometimes unsuitable, habitat – on high ground for instance, where not only could the available feed be less than ideal, but they are also more vulnerable to predation from stoats, weasels, raptors and corvids such as crows and magpies.

Water shrews

Water shrews are smaller than voles and are further identified by their sharp-pointed muzzles. They are always hungry and eat insects, worms or indeed almost any animal food. Surprisingly for such an innocent-looking creature, despite their size, they can be fierce and aggressive towards other animals and will, according to some naturalists, attack full-grown frogs 'which they do not bother to kill, but eat alive… They can dive and swim well under water, where they hunt for, and devour, caddis fly larvae' (source: *What to Look For in Spring* – see Bibliography).

DIVIDED OPINIONS ON OTTERS

Most would say that the strengthening otter population throughout Britain is a 'good thing', but there are others, mainly those in charge of fish management or involved in small mammal conservation, who might disagree. It is nowadays reckoned that there are otters in every county of the UK – a far cry from 40 years or so ago when their numbers were very much on the decrease due to organophosphate poisoning as a result of farming chemicals leeching into the waterways, including ditches.

Although they live and hunt mainly on the larger stretches of flowing water, a network of well-maintained, unpolluted drainage ditches are the otter equivalent of a motorway system and allow them to travel far more easily between their preferred streams and rivers.

INVASIVE SPECIES

Some plants and animals are definitely not wanted along the ditch – or anywhere else in the countryside for that matter – due to their proliferation endangering the welfare and natural habitat of our indigenous species. Most are the result of introductions from other countries. Take, for instance, the examples of rhododendrons (now a particular nuisance in many places such Scotland, the New Forest and elsewhere) and Japanese knotweed – both of which were brought back to the UK by interested but somewhat naïve Victorian travellers and collectors. Sometimes, though, species detrimental to the countryside's flora and fauna arrive somewhat mysteriously – the quagga mussel is a recent example.

Found in the latter part of 2014 in the River Wraybury near Heathrow airport, how exactly the quagga mussel arrived there is unknown. What is known, though, is that it is a prolific breeder and a definite threat to Britain's native freshwater mussels due to the simple fact that it suffocates them by climbing on their backs and pushing them into the silt or sediment. It also filters and cleans water – a fact which might be advantageous one might suppose. However, in doing so, it allows light to penetrate and nuisance weeds to grow and flourish.

Realising their potential danger, biologists have already developed a 'BioBullet' which will hopefully eradicate the quagga, or at least keep it under control. The 'bullet' is made up of similar material to that which this type of mussel eats, but also contains salt which causes an osmotic shock that kills them. Sadly such solutions (no pun intended) are not available for every troublesome species.

Whilst native mussels such as these are welcomed (not least because some provide a tasty meal!), the quagga is to be eradicated at all cost.

REPORTABLE NON-NATIVE SPECIES

As well as the quagga mussel, the zebra mussel, the alarmingly named killer shrimp, and two plants – floating pennywort and the water primrose – are definitely not wanted in Britain's waterways and any sign of them should be reported to the GB Non-Native Species Secretariat who can be contacted via their website: *www.nonnativespecies.org*

A direct link shows examples of the species concerned and can be found at: *www.nonnativespecies.org/ checkcleandry/non-native-species-to-look-out-for.cfm*

UNDESIRABLE PLANTS…

Japanese knotweed is, in the 21st century, causing damage to many waterways, as well as to the whole countryside in general. Amazingly, it will regenerate from pieces as small as 2 cm (0.8 in.) in soil or in water and, in the UK, this weed is one of a number listed under Schedule 9 of the 1981 *Wildlife and Countryside Act*, it being an offence in the UK to plant it or otherwise cause it to grow. It can be effectively eradicated by repeated cutting and burning. Depending on exactly where it's growing, it might also be possible to rotovate the root system, which should be raked and burnt in situ, thereby avoiding possible repercussions under the Act which also states that it is an offence to transport Japanese knotweed. Scientists are hoping psyllids – insects that devour Japanese knotweed but leave other crops or flowers untouched – will also be able to help control the spread of the plant.

People who fail to control the spread of invasive non-native plants such as Japanese knotweed could even receive anti-social behaviour orders (ASBOs) under new government rules which declare that they can be fined up to £2,500 for failing to control it and other plants such as Himalayan balsam and giant hogweed. Late to the party in telling us what many country-dwellers and naturalists have known for ages, in 2014 the Home Office went on record as saying 'these plants threaten the UK's biodiversity by crowding out native species and de-stabilising river banks'.

New Zealand pygmy-weed

New Zealand pygmy-weed is an aquatic plant native to Australia and New Zealand and was introduced to Europe through the aquarium and horticultural trades. Since it was first noticed in 1956, it has spread rapidly throughout lowland Britain. It grows all year round, is considered aggressively invasive, and, due to its vigorous growth, is more than capable of blocking drainage ditches. Difficult to eradicate using herbicides because the spray often fails to penetrate the thick mats formed by the plant, shading with black plastic sheeting for several months can be successful over small areas but it is obviously impractical where the terrain is uneven or livestock present. Mechanical removal is not recommended either as there is a tendency for fragments of stem to become detached and transferred to new areas via, for example, operators' boots, equipment or machinery.

Himalayan balsam

Himalayan balsam has been around for a long time, particularly in the south. When my children were small in the 1980s, there was never a July walk along the riverbank that didn't involve stopping off and flicking the pods of the flower in order to listen to the 'pop' and see the ripened seeds shoot out from the parent plant. In doing so, we were, of course, guilty of aiding and abetting this particular foreign undesirable plant. Quick-growing, it smothers native plants, destroys the habitat of creatures such as water voles and causes bank erosion. Fortunately there are people far more re-

The popping pods of Himalayan balsam. (Photo: Philip Halling/ Wikimedia Commons)

sponsible than me and my family, and many local wildlife/ conservation groups and fishing societies are claiming a considerable amount of success in eradicating Himalayan balsam from their waterways and ditches. Although undoubtedly invasive, it is arguably one of the least worrying plant species as far as being potentially poisonous or harmful to animals and humans.

Giant hogweed

Whilst Himalayan balsam might arguably be one of the least troublesome of invasive species, the same most certainly cannot be said of giant hogweed – I most certainly would not want my children (or anyone else's for that matter) touching this particular plant in any shape or form. It can burn the skin, cause a rash and/or make some people extremely ill. Make sure you know what it looks like and avoid contact with this plant at all costs.

Ragwort

Ragwort is a toxic plant which poses a threat to many forms of livestock (although deer are supposedly less prone to its ill effects than are domestic livestock). The *Weeds Act 1959* and the *Ragwort Control Act 2003* merely give local authorities the power to order its control in specific areas and, contrary to popular opinion, it is not otherwise illegal to have it growing on your land. Even so, it does no-one any good whatsoever and should not be allowed to grow unchecked. Whilst there are weed-killers which will destroy it, the surest remedy is to pull it up and burn it, especially when growing on the ditch side where there is a good chance that the spray from a weed-killer will find its way into the water source.

Although at the moment only of any serious concern to commercial farmers and growers of beans and peas, because the varieties of wild vetch are members of the pea family, orobanche may possibly eventually prove a

With many, if not all of the above plant species, while the recommendations are to burn invasive plants in situ, not everything is, if you'll forgive the pun, all clear-cut. *Section 40 of the Wildlife Act 1976, incorporating section 46 of the Wildlife (Amendment) Act 2000* imposes some restrictions – and allows some exceptions:

Subsection (1)

(a) *It shall be an offence* for a person to cut, grub, burn or otherwise destroy, during the period beginning on the 1st day of March and ending on the 31st day of August in any year, any vegetation growing on any land not then cultivated.

(b) *It shall be an offence* for a person to cut grub, burn or otherwise destroy any vegetation growing in any hedge or ditch during the period mentioned in paragraph (a) of this subsection.

(2) Subsection (1) of this section shall *not* apply in relation to – (a) the destroying, in the ordinary course of agriculture or forestry, of any vegetation growing on or in any hedge or ditch;

(b) the cutting or grubbing of isolated bushes or clumps or gorse, furze or whin or the mowing of isolated growths or fern in the ordinary course of agriculture;

(c) the cutting, grubbing or destroying of vegetation in the course of any works being duly carried out for reasons of public health or safety by a Minister or the Government or a body established or regulated by or under a statute;

(cc) the clearance of vegetation in the course of fisheries development works carried out by the Central Fisheries Board or a regional fisheries board in the exercise of its functions under the Fisheries Acts, 1959 to 1999;

(d) the destroying of any noxious weed to which the Noxious Weeds Act 1936, applies.

threat to the countryside in general and to ditch vegetation in particular. Orobanche has only very recently been known in Britain but it seeds prolifically (several thousand tiny seeds to one stem and 16 stems to the average plant). It is a parasitic plant which, as it is completely lacking in chlorophyll, is dependent on other plants for its necessary nutrients. The individual picking of weeds by hand is very important as the plant is

Ragwort should be pulled and burnt to prevent further spread.

Very few animals are as undesirable along the ditch as are American mink – first introduced into Britain in the 1920s. (Photo: Brendan Lally/Wikimedia Commons)

able to continue living as only a stem and produce a flower that can spread seeds even while not connected to the host.

... AND UNDESIRABLE ANIMALS

Very few animals are as undesirable along the ditch as is the American (as opposed to the European) mink, which was introduced into Britain in order to be farmed for its fur. Any efforts to get rid of this insidious menace have to be a good thing, as they have done untold damage to native wild stocks of birds and animals throughout the whole of the UK since escaping or being deliberately released from mink farms 30 years or so ago. They use small streams and ditches to travel to and fro and will, as they do so, predate on fish, many indigenous (and often rare) small mammals and the eggs, chicks and adults of waterfowl species. They can also be commercially damaging when they come into contact with animals which are being captively reared such as farmed salmon, game birds and poultry. While a nuisance throughout Britain as a whole, it seems that mink are posing a considerable problem in Scotland, particularly on the Western Isles of Harris and Lewis, and also some Hebridean islands where they have caused widespread, whole-colony breeding failures and declines in the numbers of seabirds due to their predation on eggs and chicks.

Like mink, coypu were introduced to Britain in the late 1920s and were farmed for their fur. The main points of introduction were Sussex, Hampshire, Devon and Norfolk. The habitats of the last county suffered badly once captive animals began to escape – although it's thought that the last ones were eradicated from there some 25 years ago. However, it is well worth mentioning in passing the coypu's effect on farming and ditches in France where, although they are controlled at every opportunity, they continue to cause problems to farmers and environmentalists alike. Because of their habit of burrowing and tunnelling into the sides of banks and ditches, coypu (known in France as 'ragadin') weaken the soil structure of the field edges and there have been several cases of subsidence when the edge has been run over by a tractor and the vehicle has overturned into the ditch and the driver killed. Less tragically but important nonetheless, being voracious herbivores, coypu can quickly strip both agricultural crops and natural vegetation.

... AND INSECTS

Not all ladybirds are good for the environment. Take, for instance, the case of the harlequin variety which was introduced into North America nearly three decades ago as a bio-control method for aphids on crops. It has subsequently found its way to Britain, the first sighting/notification being in September 2004. The main cause for concern is the fact that it doesn't restrict its diet to harmful aphids but will also predate on numerous beneficial insects, butterfly eggs and even other species of ladybirds.

... AND FISH

As far as unwanted types of fish are concerned, topmouth gudgeon have been in some waterways since the 1980s. It is, though, only recently that their numbers have dramatically increased and the species become widely spread – so much so, that the Environment Agency are removing native species of fish from some places before then poisoning this particular type of gudgeon with a piscicide known as 'Rotenone' (a naturally occurring organic substance that does not affect mammals or birds).

Although small, the topmouth is reckoned to be a 'significant threat' to the ecology and wildlife in UK waters due to the fact that it is able to dominate a habitat and food supply. They are also reckoned to carry infections and parasites which can wipe out entire populations of native fish.

FLORA AND FAUNA CONSERVATION GROUPS

Incredibly, according to a report released in late 2013, nearly four and a half million people (or 1 in 10 UK adults) are now members or supporters of Britain's many and varied environment and conservation groups, so we are obviously not alone in our love of ditches and the countryside – nor are we the only ones worrying about its future (of which more in Chapter 7).

There are a whole host of conservation groups. One of these has the umbrella title of The Wildlife Trusts but in actual fact, there are 47 regional off-shoots covering the whole of the UK. Each is an independent charity which, as their website says: 'is deeply-rooted within the local communities from which it was formed… [M]ost had been established by the end of the 1960s (usually, but not always, at a county-wide level), often set up by local activists determined to save what they could – the last remaining meadows, ancient woods, heaths – in the face of widespread devastation to our natural environment.' Furthermore, as a whole, they are 'the UK's largest people-powered environmental organisation working for nature's recovery on land and at sea'.

The Wildlife Trusts logo is well known and eagerly followed by many conservation volunteers and naturalists.

The Joint Nature Conservation Committee quite rightly believes that Britain's natural environment and its biodiversity provides a vital and valuable role in supporting the basic natural services upon which we all depend, such as food, fresh water and clean air. They cite, as an example, the fact that 'bees pollinate our crops and the crops in turn provide us with food' and further mention that 'nature conservation… maintain[s] and enrich[es] our biodiversity'.

As far as interested amateur naturalists are concerned, there is arguably no better group to which to belong than The Conservation Volunteers. The organisation originally began under the banner of the Conservation Corps before switching to the revamped title of the British Trust for Conservation Volunteers (BTCV), before then undergoing a second change of identity in 2000, taking the initials BTCV as its new name in full. In May 2012, the BTCV was rebranded under the trading name of The Conservation Volunteers and at the group's AGM later in the same year, members voted unanimously to change formally the name of the charity to The Conservation Volunteers.

More specialised groups of undoubted interest to the ditch-watcher and conservationist are the British Dragonfly Society and the Canal and River Trust, but there are certainly plenty more with which one might like to become involved.

NATURALISTS AND CONSERVATIONISTS

Even before the formation of various conservation groups, there have long been amateur naturalists of note. While the Victorian and Edwardian writers such as Richard Jefferies and Edith Holden (famous for her nature notes in *The Country Diary of an Edwardian Lady*) and even Beatrix Potter observing animal life (much of it in a ditch… think *The Tale of Jeremy Fisher!*) did much to educate and inform, it was the naturalists of the mid-20th century or thereabouts that did most. Many of these came to the attention of the public through the relatively new medium of radio – and as a result, reached a far wider audience than anyone had ever previously done with their note-taking and book writing.

George Bramwell Evans, better known as 'Romany', was a religious minister who just happened to have a love of both nature and his native Cumbria. Famous as the author of many books describing life living in a gypsy caravan with his dog Raq, he was also the presenter of *Out with Romany*, a long-running series on radio's *Children's Hour* and is, in fact, often credited as being Britain's first ever wildlife presenter.

Listeners to his broadcasts were encouraged to believe that they were 'real life rambles' in which he met and chatted to country people whilst travelling the highways and by-ways with his caravan and dog – but it was all smoke and mirrors as in reality, the programmes were recorded in a Manchester studio. Not that the people he talked to were not genuine country folk; it was more the practicalities of transmission that dictated a studio situation rather than an outside broadcast as would be done today.

For some reason far less well known, Eric Simms was, nevertheless, an eminent ornithologist and noted amateur authority on bird migration, writing more than 20 books on the subject. For many years the presenter of BBC Radio's *The Countryside*, Simms was, possibly more importantly, also a ground-breaking wildlife sound recordist. Unlike the producers of the *Out with Romany* programmes, he took all the equipment and paraphernalia necessary outdoors to record birdsong and other natural sounds. Not only that, he was the first person to record wildlife on

Naturalist and radio broadcaster George Bramwell Evans (aka 'Romany') would travel the by-ways of Britain in a gypsy caravan (somewhat more muted in colour than this particular example!) in the company of his dog Raq. (*Photo: courtesy of Sue Smith/David Shepherd*)

magnetic tape and pioneered the use of portable tape recorders and radio links in an outdoors situation.

Alongside 'Romany', another well-known countryside radio celebrity of the time was Walter Flesher. Despite having lost an arm at Passendaele during the First World War, Flesher was, for over quarter of a century, a grouse moor keeper on Burley Moor in Yorkshire. However, such was his immense knowledge of natural history, he was approached by the powers that be to broadcast on *Children's Hour* under the pseudonym of 'Ted Brock the Gamekeeper' where he passed on his acquired knowledge to several generations. Eventually, as the medium of television developed, he also began to appear on screen with other eminent naturalists such as Sir Peter Scott.

Other writers and naturalists whose names are still remembered by many of today's countryside lovers and inhabitants include A. G. Street, Henry Williamson (possibly most famous for his book *Tarka*), H. J. Massingham and Adrian Bell. To most of my generation, though, it is probably Jack Hargreaves who everyone thinks of in connection with educating and informing the populace about nature and the countryside. Known to most for his much loved and hugely successful *Out of Town* series on Southern Television which was first aired in 1963, Hargreaves was, however, a radio presenter in the 1930s and was, alongside the likes of 'Romany', Walter Flesher and others of immediate pre- and post-war years, the forerunner of the likes of Chris Packham, Matt Baker and Michaela Strachan presenting programmes such as *Countryfile* and *Springwatch*.

So, every generation has had its influential naturalists without whose findings and observations we would all be much the poorer, and it somehow seems appropriate to end this chapter by mentioning just one more. Denys Watkins-Pitchford was a British writer and countryman who mainly wrote under the *nom de plume* of 'BB'. A prolific author with almost 60 titles to his credit – and an artist of no mean repute – he had, at the beginning of every one of his books, a woodcut illustration of a cowslip (a very definite springtime flower of the ditch banks), together with the following verse:

The wonder of the world
The beauty and the power
The shape of things,
Their colours, lights and shades,
These I saw.
Look ye also while life lasts.

Taking all that into consideration, what exactly might the interested amateur discover and observe in a ditch during any given month of the year? The next chapter ambles through the calendar months in order to 'look ye also while life lasts'.

4

A YEAR IN THE LIFE OF A DITCH

The Romans only had ten months in their year – which began on March 25th. Eventually, however, Britain began using the Julian calendar – a very strange system wherein there were 12 months of 30 days and a 13th one of five. However, despite its complications, it appears that the system was popular enough, and when the changeover to the calendar devised by Pope Gregory XIII in the late 1500s was mooted, there was public outcry throughout the British Isles, with people demanding that they should be given back their 'lost' days!

The Gregorian calendar was implemented at different times throughout Britain. Scotland was the first and, in 1599, the Privy Council there resolved that the following year should officially begin on January 1st. In Wales and the majority of England it was, though, as late as 1752 before the calendar as we know it was in common usage. And, should you have a mind for trivia, the Latin word 'Calendae' means the first day of the month, so it would appear that there's a definite link between that and the English word 'calendar'!

SEASONAL SIGHTINGS

As far as the casual ditch-watcher is concerned, it is perhaps the seasons rather than the calendar dates which are more relevant. Nonetheless, the astronomical calendar (as opposed to the meteorological one) has it that spring falls between March and May; summer, June to August; autumn, September to November; and winter, December to February. Unfortunately, no-one remembered to tell the flowers and wildlife who detect the changing seasons more by weather conditions than they do a glossy wall-mounted almanac.

The media-loved expression, 'the North/South Divide', can apply to the habitat and inhabitants of a typical ditch as much as it does to human house prices and commodity costs. Generally (but not always – as recent winters have shown), the weather is warmer in the south of the country and the emergence of spring plants and the breeding cycles of insects, birds and mammals may well begin a week or so earlier than in the north. For this reason, the division of the likely happenings in and around a ditch over a 12-month period cannot always be exact. What follows is, though, near enough for our purposes!

JANUARY

It's unlikely that, apart from a brisk walk along its banks whilst exercising the dog, you will be tempted towards the ditch at this time of year – and if you are, you'll probably not want to linger anywhere near as long as you might in summer. Cold though it may be, the movement of water and the fractionally higher temperature afforded by secluded banks and overhanging tree branches does, however, make the location slightly more attractive to plants, birds and animals, even if there's little appreciable difference to humans.

A BIRD IN THE BUSH

In certain secluded areas, lesser celandines should be showing now and the catkins ought to be obvious on the hazel branches. Bird-wise, reed buntings, song thrushes and chiffchaffs might be seen and heard. It's also not too early for some of them to be thinking about gathering nesting material – particularly long-tailed tits, which construct a domed nest, densely packed with feathers and covered in lichen. From start to finish, it might take these birds nearly a month to build a nest – which is often sited in the relatively low undergrowth (such as bramble) growing along the ditch bank.

Sometimes a wintery, watery sun in January puts an unexpected, spring-like slant on things for plants, birds and humans – as T. S. Eliot noted in his first verse of *Little Gidding*:

> Midwinter spring is its own season
> Sempiternal though sodden towards sundown,
> Suspended in time, between pole and tropic.
> When the short day is brightest, with frost and fire,
> The brief sun flames the ice, on pond and ditches,
> In windless cold that is the heart's heat,
> Reflecting in a watery mirror
> A glare that is blindness in the early afternoon.

Even in January, some winter sunshine can make a ditch a very pleasant place in which to spend some time.

LOOK OUT FOR:

* Frog spawn can appear as early as the New Year in a mild winter, although cold, heavy weather may delay its appearance until spring – the time we most associate with frog spawn. Frogs and toads will quickly disappear out of sight on being disturbed but if you sit or crouch quietly on the bankside for a few minutes, such is their ardour during the breeding season, it will not be very long before they reappear.

* Kingfishers prefer stretches of more open, straighter watercourses than are generally offered by ditches but, having said that, one can occasionally be glimpsed in such places whilst on the look-out for small fish. Once caught, its prey is most commonly stunned by being beaten on a convenient branch or post before being eaten, head-first – the reason being that, were a kingfisher to attempt swallowing a fish tail-end first, it would find it very difficult due to the open fins and rough scales of the fish.

Frogs will quickly disappear out of sight on being disturbed but if you crouch quietly on the bank side for a few minutes, such is their ardour during the breeding season that it will not be very long before they reappear. (Photo: courtesy of Helen Tait-Wright)

FEBRUARY

It is impossible not to mention the proverb 'February fill-dyke/be it black or white/but if it be white/it's the better to like' in a book about ditches! The 'black' alluded to indicates rain water whilst the 'white' tells of melting snow. Why the latter should have been thought any better than the former, I've been unable to establish – maybe it is because the water produced from snow is cleaner and purer than the sort running through the ditch as a result of run-off from the muddy fields? Whatever the reason, Worcester artist Benjamin Williams Leader painted one of the most famous images of a February country landscape in his painting *February Fill Dyke* which was, when initially exhibited at the Royal Academy, not very well received by the critics but has proved extremely popular with many generations since. The painting can nowadays be seen at the Birmingham Art Gallery.

DOUBLE CHANCE OF SUCCESS

Mallard are stupid things – or perhaps not! They pair up early in the year and by February the female may even be sitting on a clutch of eggs in a nest made on the bankside of a ditch. I suggest that they might be stupid for several reasons: (a) because sudden flooding may force the duck to abandon her nest; (b) a scarcity of natural cover at this time of year leaves the nest vulnerable to magpies and crows, and (c) should any ducklings hatch out, there is little in the way of insects and other natural food for them to eat. On the other hand, why mallard might not be all that stupid is the fact that, with such an early start to their breeding season, if they are successful, all well and good but, if not, there's ample opportunity to lay a second clutch later in the spring.

While still on the topic of mallard, it is well known amongst country-dwellers and naturalists that male mallard are aggressive during the breeding season – and that several will gang up on a single female in order to mate with her. Less well known are their homosexual tendencies. On at least one occasion, necrophilia has been added to this list – as documented by a Dutch researcher and subsequently reported in the *Guardian* newspaper in March 2005.

The researcher, a certain Mr Moeliker, was working in his office at the Natural History Museum in Rotterdam, when he was alerted by a bang to the fact a bird had crashed into the glass facade of the building:

> I went downstairs immediately to see if the window was damaged, and saw a drake mallard lying motionless on its belly... The unfortunate duck apparently had hit the building in full flight... Next to the obviously dead duck, another male mallard... was present. He forcibly pecked into the back, the base of the bill and mostly into the back of the head of the dead mallard for about two minutes, then mounted the corpse and started to copulate, with great force, almost continuously pecking the side of the head.

> Rather startled, I watched this scene from close quarters behind the window... during which time (75 minutes) I made some photographs [as] the mallard almost continuously copulated with his dead congener.

Male mallard are notoriously aggressive during the breeding season. (Photo: Joe Mabel/Wikimedia Commons)

LOOK OUT FOR:

* Training days on how to help a toad cross the road? Yes really! At this time of year, the Amphibian and Reptile Conservation Trust, along with local conservation groups, organise such days in order to raise awareness of the plight of our common toads in preparation for their migration to breeding ponds in early spring.

* Should you happen to be out and about in the early morning and follow a ditch bank along which a hedge or trees grow, there's a good chance that you'll hear the beginnings of a dawn chorus. Whilst songbirds don't really get into their stride vocally until next month, a mild morning often fools them into thinking that spring has sprung!

* On a fine, warm day, listen out for the drumming of woodpeckers as they search for insects that have been overwintering underneath the bark of tall trees. They also drum to protect their territory at the beginning of the breeding season – but don't get the headache one might assume because of the fact their beaks are protected by tissue that acts in a similar way to a car's shock absorbers.

* Some early spring flowers ought to start appearing around now. Being a lover of the water's edge, the lesser celandine is an obvious one but others include the marsh marigold which, if it doesn't appear now, most certainly will next month.

MAR**CH**

Herons generally build their nests in a heronry amongst high trees. They will, though, use any shallow-banked (herons prefer to walk into water) ditches as a food source. Moorhens build a nesting platform of dried water plants in or near the edge of a wide ditch (they will probably not choose a narrow, steep-banked, heavily vegetated one as it would be likely to leave them more vulnerable to predators), and whilst they can be seen pottering around the water margins at any time of the year, it is towards the end of this month that they generally begin to nest – although nests and chicks can often be seen right up to, and including, July. The chicks can swim and dive immediately they leave the nest and are fed by both parents – and sometimes even the young from a previous brood.

PROMINENT PRIMROSES

Celandines like the banks of a particularly damp ditch – but primroses

The lesser celandine emerging on the banks of a ditch or similar inland waterway is a sure sign of spring being just around the corner. The poet Wordsworth was as much a fan of these little flowers as he more famously was of daffodils!

> Pansies, lilies, kingcups, daisies,
> Let them live upon their praises;
> Long as there's a sun that sets,
> Primroses will have their glory;
> Long as there are violets,
> They will have a place in story:
> There's a flower that shall be mine,
> 'Tis the little Celandine…
> Ill befall
> The yellow flowers,
> Children of the flaring hours!
> Buttercups, that will be seen,
> Whether we will see or no;
> Other, too, of lofty mien;
> They have done as worldings do,
> Take praise that should be thine,
> Little, humble Celandine!

Celandine emerging on the banks of a ditch or similar inland waterway are a sure sign of spring being just around the corner.

Moorhen chicks can swim and dive immediately they leave the nest.
(Photo: courtesy of Helen Tait-Wright)

seem to prefer the banksides of those which are slightly drier and less susceptible to flooding (arguably, roadside ditches are their favourite place – provided that they are not polluted by salt spread on the road over winter, or by excessive car exhaust fumes). E. L. Grant Wilson, in his text for *What to Look For in Spring* (Ladybird Books, 1961), has it that there are two kinds of primrose flowers: 'one has long stamens and a short pistil, and the other has short stamens and a long pistil which reaches to the top of the tube made by the petals and calyx. These two kinds ensure cross-fertilisation.'

LOOK OUT FOR:

* Little or no foliage makes it slightly easier to see birds at this time of year rather than, as will be the case in a month or two's time, just hear them!
* Hedgehogs emerge from their winter hibernation, especially on mild sunny spring days; likewise, bumblebees can be seen buzzing around on the warmer days and ladybirds also start to appear from places where they've spent the winter.
* New shoots of winter heliotrope might be flowering in March.
* Queen bumblebees wake up from hibernation any time around now – and need to feed on any available ditch-side flowers in order to gain energy before laying eggs. Look out for them on sunny, spring-like days.
* By the spring equinox (towards the end of this month) many ditch residents, including small mammals, amphibians and insects, will have already either given birth or laid spawn and eggs, whilst many more will be about to do so.
* Mistle thrushes, especially, will make good use of any mature ivy berries still to be found on trees growing in a hedge that is situated on the bank of a ditch.

Even if not seen feeding on ivy berries, evidence of mistle thrushes might be found in the shape of snail shells left at the base of a stone, post or tree stump.

TOAD IN THE HOLE

Although they will most often be found in ditches or under wet vegetation outdoors, it seems that, at one time, toads could be found in churches – and what's more, were fed by the congregation! In his book *Afoot in England* (1909), the famous country writer and naturalist W. H. Hudson wrote that he had visited a very damp West Country church which was, according to the vicar, 'haunted by toads'. This erstwhile clergyman then went on to say:

> … during my first year… I discovered it was the custom here to keep pet toads in the church… all the best people in the parish had one of these creatures, and it was customary for the ladies to bring it a weekly supply of provisions – bits of meat, hard-boiled eggs chopped up, and earthworms and whatever else they fancied it would like… The toads, I suppose, knew when it was Sunday – their feeding day; at all events they would crawl out of their holes in the floor under the pews to receive their rations.

APRIL

Most country kids (certainly of my generation) will have spent some of their springtime paddling about in streams and ditches in search of stickleback fish. Some of us might never have left childhood behind and whilst I no longer go out equipped with a small net and a jam-jar around the neck of which my father would have tightly tied a piece of string in order to form a carrying-handle, I must admit that, at this time of year, should I happen to see sticklebacks, their sighting gives me just as much pleasure now as it did then!

> Sometimes as the children paddle up the stream they see a brown cloud in the water, darting up and up before them in swift swimming jerks... and watch the shoal of little fishes flashing through the water just out of reach of them. From moment to moment one of them turns half over in the water, with a flash of silver as he turns. And sometimes, when the children are all lying on the bank, we see the shoal swim slowly past us, and watch them fling themselves right out of the water after the tiny flies that play over the surface of the stream. Then it is as if a clever juggler were hidden under the water and were throwing little curved knives up from the bottom of the stream to twist and sparkle in the air, and then fall plosh, plosh, into widening circles of ripples... [Fish after fish] leaps out of the water, turns and falls, and the ripples of the different splashes cross one another and cut the water into a thousand glittering points of light.
> (Arthur Ransome, Pond and Stream, 1906)

A CUCKOO IN SPRING

Despite not being as common in Britain as they once were, April is the month to first hear cuckoos. They are interesting birds: John Clare began one of his poems with the line, 'The cuckoo like a hawk in flight' and, almost 200 years after he wrote those words, researchers at Cambridge University discovered that cuckoos behave so similarly to birds of prey (particularly sparrow-hawks) that they can scare songbirds from their nests. Well known for laying their eggs in other birds' nests (a practice known to biologists and ornithologists as 'brood parasitism'), cuckoos seem to favour three particular types of birds as foster-parents to their young: the meadow pipit, the dunnock and, of great interest to the ditch-watcher in certain parts of the country, the reed warbler. Apparently, cuckoos will, given a choice, always lay in the nests of the same species which raised them... as I say, interesting birds!

LOOK OUT FOR:

* Throughout all the other seasons, both male and female sticklebacks look virtually the same but, in April (their typical breeding time), the male turns brighter in colour and has a reddish 'chest'.
* Being night creatures, brook lampreys are rarely seen except at spawning time (this month and next) when they move into shallow, clear water during daylight to start their complex, communal nest-building activities involving the gathering of stones. Look out for them in places where there are stones and gravel where a water current is present but not overly strong.
* Common throughout Britain, the green-veined white butterfly frequents damp regions – and is one of the first species to be seen in the spring.
* Spring has truly sprung when you see cowslips on the ditch bank, wild garlic in the shaded, damp places leading to it, and bluebells in the woods beyond!

Spring has truly sprung when you see cowslips on the ditch bank!

MAY

Yellow flag irises love the boggy areas of a ditch and flower in May. I know this for a fact! Difficult though it might be to believe now that there are 24/7 shopping outlets within easy reach of almost any-where, back in 1980, when my son was born at the end of May on an early Sunday morning, it was im-possible to find a florist (or even a garage) open and so, rather than visit my wife empty-handed when I went back to visit her in the evening, I had to resort to stopping the car by a rural ditch and cut a bunch of flag iris with my penknife. Needless to say, my muddy shoes received some quizzical (and disapproving) looks from the hospital staff!

It was probably against the *Wildlife and Countryside Act* to have picked even something as common as flag irises – pick wild orchids and one would most definitely be committing an offence. Once quite rare, wild orchids are now seen quite readily in the damp places along a ditch side or shady hedgerow.

OBSERVING OTTERS

Otters generally mate in the spring and give birth from May onwards, the young often staying with their mothers until the following year when they wander off down the drainage ditches, streams and other river tributaries in search of a mate.

Wild orchids: now far more common than they once were, but still very much a protected species.

Almost wiped out during the 20th century through a combination of pesticide poisoning and habitat destruction, otters are now once again on the increase, thanks to the improvement of rivers and waterways, the banning of harmful pesticides and numerous conservation projects across the country. So much have their fortunes changed that it is reckoned that otters inhabit almost every British county, so there's every chance that one might be spotted along the length of a ditch. (See also 'Divided opinions on otters' on page 56.)

ALDER – A CURE FOR INFLAMMATION

The common alder grows well in watery places – it flowers during April and May, and yields seed in September. Nicholas Culpeper mentioned its various uses in his famous book *Culpeper's Complete Herbal*, first published in 1653:

> ... the decoction or distilled water of the leaves is excellent against burnings and inflammation ... and especially for that inflammation in the breast which the vulgar call an ague... The leaves and bark of the alder-tree are cooling, drying and binding. The fresh leaves laid upon swellings dissolves them, and stays the inflammations; the leaves, put under the bare feet galled with travelling, are a great refreshment to them, and brought into a chamber troubled with fleas, will gather them thereinto, which, being suddenly cast out, will rid the chamber of these troublesome bed-fellows.

LOOK OUT FOR:

* The first mayflies appear (somewhat unsurprisingly!) in May and provide a useful food source to many fish and songbirds that inhabit wetlands, marshes and ditches.
* Great-crested newts breed about now, unlike frogs and toads which began their courtship rituals several weeks ago.
* Water crowfoot thrives in the clearer ditches and provides shelter for many insects – so it may be well worth examining!

* Of all the spring flowers, the fritillaries just have to be the most delicate and beautiful: they thrive in wet areas – particularly those that periodically flood.

* Marsh fritillary butterflies are common enough in some areas but in others have become quite scarce – due, it is thought, to the land drainage that occurred a few decades ago. Where they are found, they can be seen on the wing in May and June.

* If you are out and about in the ditch as dusk falls – and don't live in Scotland (where, I believe, it is absent) – it might, in the late spring/early summer, be possible to notice examples of the eyed hawk moth which feeds on willows and sallow growing in damp areas. The narrow-bordered bee hawk moth frequents rough pastures, marshy land and open, easily accessible ditches and is a daytime rather than night-time flyer.

Great-crested newts breed about now – and appear on the postage stamps of Russia and Belarus!

There can be few pieces of writing more evocative of a sunny early summer's day at the edge of a rural meadow than this – written by children's author, Arthur Ransome, in 1906:

A little farther down the stream a broad deep ditch crosses the meadows to join it. The ditch is deep, and the water in it moves so slowly that it is almost still. Weeds and grasses grow from the bottom of the stream, and are only just bent over by the current, and the moist edges of the ditch are full of sunken holes, where the cows have thrust their feet into the mud. The whole of the ground by the side of the ditch is rich with flowers, but so swampy that they are difficult to reach, except at a few places.

JUNE

By June, it should be possible to see some of the many varieties of damselflies and dragonflies which, up until recent years at least, are normally found around the edges of any stretch of fresh water throughout the UK. Why their numbers might be diminishing in certain areas is explained in the previous chapter but, assuming that your particular stretch of ditch has remained unaffected by flooding, the only problem for the amateur ditch-watcher is how to differentiate between the two groups.

For the scientifically and technically minded, both apparently belong to the order *Odonata* – all of which share certain characteristics such as membranous wings, large eyes, slender bodies, and small antennae. To the casual amateur, one of the most obvious differences between the two groups are the fact that dragonflies generally have eyes that touch – or nearly touch – at the top of the head, whereas the eyes of a damselfly are clearly separated and show quite definitely as being to the sides of the head. Another major difference is that, when resting, a dragonfly holds its wings invitingly open, either horizontally or vertically, but the damselfly is rather coy about such things and places its wings close tight over its abdomen. As a personal aside, I would also add that damselflies are generally the smaller of the two... but you need both close to hand in order to compare!

The large red damselfly is one of the earliest to appear each year. It dislikes fast-flowing streams and rivers so is quite at home in a ditch environment. (Photo: courtesy of Helen Tait-Wright)

BLANKET COVERAGE

Some ditches (particularly slow-running ones) might be overgrown with algae, duck-weed or blanket-weed by now. The amount of growth is an indicator of what's happening to the water content as, whilst some of this type of growth is normal and to be expected, too much may well be a result of 'background' pollution. Examples include a run-off of fertilisers, silage, farmyard activities or even surplus water from a nearby road.

Emergent growth such as bulrush, reed mace and common reed may also begin to choke a ditch at this time of year. Growing in the marginal shallows of a relatively deep ditch, they offer valuable wildlife habitat but when the ditch is shallow across the whole of its base, they can tend to take over and completely fill it – at which point, only a very limited amount of wildlife will benefit.

LOOK OUT FOR:

* Drinker moths like damp areas – and are on the wing between now and August. Blood vein moths are most frequently seen in June, particularly in roadside ditches, field margins and hedgerows. The scarlet tiger moth – generally only seen in southern England and south-west Wales – is a daytime flier and might well be noticed on the banks of a ditch or small stream and in any fenland-type areas. Open ditches, on the roadside for example, are a favourite place for the marbled white butterfly – and it's often possible to see family colonies grouped together.
* Water and wetlands can be excellent feeding grounds for bats, particularly during the early summer when water-loving insects hatch off and are plentiful.
* On a fine evening, watch swallows and swifts as they hawk for insects high over the ditch. The reason for their height is that the insects are wafted upwards by the warm thermal currents.
* This month and next is the 'peak season' for glow worms – fascinating creatures; especially the female who produces the bright, luminous green light from which they derive their name.
* Grass snakes like to live near water and will lay their eggs in clumps of rotting waterside vegetation; the young from these eggs emerge during the summer months.

Emergent growth such as bulrush, reed mace and common
reed may begin to choke a ditch at this time of year.

Open ditches are a favourite place for the marbled white butterfly and it is not uncommon to see family groups clustered together.

'WHAT TO LOOK FOR...'

Those of us who were at primary school in the early 1960s will all no doubt remember the 'Ladybird' series of books which dealt with what went on in the countryside during the four seasons. Written by E. L. Grant Watson and beautifully illustrated by C. F. Tunnicliffe, the series began in 1959 with *What to Look For in Winter*, and was followed each year afterwards by *...Summer*, *...Spring* and *...Autumn*.

The text was informative and educational (for both child and adult) and Tunnicliffe's illustrations, beautiful and evocative works of art. Even now, when I stand at some countryside vantage point 50-plus years later, I find myself saying: 'That is just like a scene in a *What to look for...* book.' Little else from my school days has ever made such a lasting impression!

JULY

Most butterfly species will have emerged by the beginning of the month. When they are adult and the beautiful thing we see in the grasses, hedgerows and ditches, they are almost at the end of their life cycle (egg, larva, pupa and adult) and, at this stage, are looking to feed, mate and lay eggs. A pair of butterflies may well perform a courtship ritual in much the same way as do some birds but it is the fact that some species excrete and send out pheromones to attract the opposite sex which I find most fascinating. In general, it is the males which do this (from glands on their wings) but in some, as David Carter points out in his excellent book, *Butterflies & Moths in Britain and Europe*: 'Prior to the final stages of mating, many female butterflies and moths are capable of attracting males by releasing their own pheromones [which are] capable of attracting males over quite long distances, up to several kilometres.' Perhaps even more interesting is the fact that although female pheromones do not seem to be detectable by humans, some male pheromones are – and may be recognised by their flower-like or fruity scents.

Whether or not they come from male butterflies or moths, the ditch can actually prove to be full of interesting smells and scents at this time of year – and I'm not talking of any that might emanate from any stagnant water at the bottom; more the flowers and grasses on the banksides.

Sweet by name, sweet by nature

Meadowsweet grows in profusion in damp meadows, on boggy stream-banks, and on pond and ditch sides throughout Britain from June to September. It is, however, in July that it is at its best – particularly when it comes to giving off its heavy fragrance from both its creamy-white flowers and large leaves. So sweet-smelling is it that, in times gone by, the plant and its flowers were cut and included amongst reeds and rushes used as floor coverings in homes in the fond belief that its pungent smell would ward off the 'noxious vapours' from street gutters, open cess-pits and kitchen middens. This somewhat naïve thinking came from the idea that diseases were carried by foul air and, by using a naturally produced fragrance, good would overcome evil. In addition, at one time, the floors of churches were made simply of loose earth and it was commonplace to bury bodies of well-to-do villagers within the church as well as in the churchyard. To guard against the smell of decaying bodies (and prevent disease), parishioners brought meadowsweet and rushes to strew within the church in order to purify the air. The ancient custom of rush-bearing still continues in many parts of Britain – in particular Cumbria, where, during the summer months, at least five churches are still strewn with wild rushes and fragrant flowers after a traditional procession around the associated villages.

Look out for:

* This is a good time to see arrowhead and water plantains, both of which have three-petalled flowers. Also at their best in July are the water forget-me-nots, water mint, gypsywort and brooklime.
* Watch where you are treading along the ditch bank: during damp weather there may be tiny froglets intent on moving away from the water and into the grass.
* Last month and this are good times to look out for glow worms after dark – and to marvel at their effervescence. Thomas Hardy, in *The Return of the Native* (1878), describes a scene where dice players, short of light for their game, collect 13 glow worms from outdoors in order to continue their playing as darkness approaches!
* With so many plant types and insect species bearing a remarkable similarity to one another it is not always possible to identify what one has seen. Books and the internet help a great deal but at this time of year it could pay to enrol on an evening's walk and talk organised by a nearby wildlife group.

AUGUST

Around the time of the harvest (from August onwards) the crane-flies (or daddy-long-legs) appear in their greatest numbers. The larval stage of this family of insects (there are many species) are commonly referred to as leather-jackets. Despite being destructive in cereal fields and elsewhere on farmland, this maggot-like larva is an important food source for many birds, both small and large. In the spring and early summer when rooks are seen in a cultivated field, they are searching for leather-jackets rather than, as is sometimes thought, pulling up the farmer's crops.

A necessary evil

If only a periodic visitor to your particular ditch, don't be surprised to find the banks shorn and the overhanging branches clipped. Farmers

The ditch in high summer.

often use the period between harvest and ploughing to carry out such chores – mainly because of the fact that, in a normal year, the ground is firm enough to take the weight of tractors and heavy machinery. The way it is carried out might not be the best or most sympathetic, but some maintenance of a ditch is undoubtedly better than none at all. 'It is notorious that hedging and ditching are amongst the rural crafts which run considerable danger of being neglected'... no, not my words, nor a quote from some 21st century conservation group; they were, in fact, a part of a *Country Life* article published way back in 1911.

All ditches will, at some stage, become overgrown and require some maintenance. Here a rudimentary 'short-back-and-sides' (particularly of the overhanging hedge) will benefit both flora and fauna in years to come.

PENNY-ROYAL… A VALUABLE HERB

There are several varieties of the herbal penny-royal, which is both a garden plant and grows wild in moist and watery places, and flowers towards the end of summer. Dioscorides, a famous physician who travelled throughout the Roman Empire with Emperor Nero's army, was of the opinion that, administered to humans, it is capable of making 'tough phlegm thin' and 'warms the coldness of any part that it is applied to, and digests raw and corrupt matter: being boiled and drunk, it removes the menses, and expels the dead child and after-birth; being mixed with honey and salt, it voids phlegm out of the lungs. Drunk with wine, it is of singular service to those who are stung or bit by any venomous beast.' In his treatise, Dioscorides goes on extolling its virtues for much longer but there's sufficient here to prove that he held penny-royal in very high esteem indeed!

LOOK OUT FOR:

* The pebble prominent moth particularly likes fenland and damp places – and is interesting in that, whilst in the north of the country they might only have one brood, in the south it is not uncommon for them to produce two, or occasionally three. The first moths can be seen flying in April but any second brood will be out and about this month – with the offspring of any third brood showing until as late as October.
* The water crowfoot will be lush and wide-spreading in the cleaner, relatively fast-flowing ditches. In places where it's slower, and therefore more silty, it is possible that yellow water lily may be present – and be in full flower.
* Although the bankside vegetation will be dense in August, there may be a very obvious track running through it. What made it might require some detective work similar to that described in the second chapter of this book – or you could position yourself downwind one evening and sit quietly in the hope of seeing what has been travelling through on a regular basis. Deer, foxes and hares will pass through with no noise at all, but the shuffling, snuffling badger will certainly advertise his arrival!

SEPTEMBER

It is, I must admit, included as a somewhat flippant remark but there is, nevertheless, an element of seriousness in the comment I'm about to make. As an avid ditch-watcher, it's quite likely that you may well find yourself straying away from public footpaths and onto private land in your personal search for the rural equivalent of the source of the Nile.

September 1st sees the start of the wild duck and partridge

SOME NOTABLE QUOTES ON NATURE

'One can never study nature too much and too hard.' – Vincent van Gogh

'Study nature, love nature, stay close to nature. It will never fail you.' – Frank Lloyd Wright

'It seems to me that we all look at nature too much, and live with her too little.' – Oscar Wilde

'Nature: a place where birds fly around uncooked.' – Oscar Wilde

shooting season in Britain and there is, therefore, always the possibility that wandering off-track might bring you somewhere where it's best not to be! The pheasant shooting season begins on the first of next month and, although there are differences in the dates that the various game-bird seasons finish, it is probably easiest to assume that they continue until February 1st. Should you be exploring ditches that meander to the foreshore, however, wildfowling continues until February 20th. If your eyes are down perusing a moorland ditch or 'grip', the grouse shooting season starts on August 12th (the 'Glorious Twelfth') and finishes on December 10th. Just to complicate matters further, boggy moorland areas are often home to snipe – and their season continues until January 31st.

Wood mouse harvest

Wood mice, despite their name, live in all manner of places, including ditch lines and nearby hedgerows. They might best be seen from now onwards as, although they don't hibernate, they do live in 'communes' during the winter and will be starting to gather seeds and the like for winter feeding. Interestingly, as they forage, they place markers such as leaves and twigs for the benefit of other wood mice – a practice which is probably safer than scent-marking when it comes to being noticed by any potential predators in the vicinity.

In the hedges and shrubs that can often be found alongside a ditch, there is quite likely to be the odd stand or two of hazel – and, some years, at this point in the season, you might be lucky enough to discover nuts ready to harvest. Provided you can get to them before the mice and squirrels, they are a healthy snack, rich in protein and an excellent source of minerals.

Look out for:

* September is the best time of year to see water voles along the ditch as their numbers are likely to be at their highest due to it being the end of the breeding season.
* The yellow flowers of bird's-foot trefoil and yellow loosestrife can often be found in amongst the dense stands of vegetation in damp marshy ground where the ditch sides have subsided.
* Provided that the weather is still good, butterflies and other summer insects should still be very much in evidence.
* If you've lost your hazel-nuts to the mice and squirrels, console yourself with a glass of elderberry wine! Widespread along any hedge that follows

a ditch, the berries of the elder make a very good traditional country wine and should be ripe enough to pick around now. Elderflowers gathered in late May/early June have long been used to make either elderflower cordial or 'champagne'.

OCTOBER

As winter rapidly approaches, the leaves fall from the trees and some animals begin to look out for suitable places in which to hibernate, there is a recognisable poignancy in the words of Kenneth Grahame writing in his children's classic *The Wind in the Willows* – in which he describes 'Nature's Grand Hotel' as having a 'season' and in the autumn, 'guests one by one pack, pay, and depart, and the seats at the table-d'hote shrink pitifully at each succeeding meal'.

HIBERNATING DORMICE

'The Dormouse had closed its eyes by this time, and was going off into a doze; but, on being pinched by the Hatter, it woke up again with a little shriek...' (Lewis Carroll, *Alice Through the Looking-glass*). Towards the

Dormice might weave a nest near the base of a hedge in preparation for a winter of hibernation. (Photo: courtesy of Phil Rant)

OCTOBER WEATHER PREDICTIONS

It is always as well to know what the weather conditions might be over the coming months – and if the ditches and waterways are likely to flood or freeze. October is a month bursting with weather sayings and traditional verse; just how reliable they could prove to be is another matter entirely!

If ducks do slide at Hallow-tide,
At Christmas they do swim;
If ducks do swim at Hallow-tide,
At Christmas they will slide.

Many weather predictions for the month seem to be based around birds. If, for example, field-fares and red-wings are seen during October, a hard winter is sure to follow. Tradition also has it that if a squirrel has a bushy tail, it indicates a cold snap: in reality, a bushy tail is an early warning system to other squirrels, but don't let that fact spoil a good story. Likewise, a plethora of fruits such as blackberries (and don't forget to pick them in early October otherwise the witches will have spat on them!) is said to indicate some inclement weather: botanical evidence, however, proves that the amount of berries on a bush or tree depends entirely on the weather conditions during the preceding spring.

Finally:

Rain in October
Gives wind in December.
If the October moon comes without frost,
Expect no frost until the moon of November.

end of the month, dormice might weave a nest near the base of a hedge in preparation for a winter of hibernation – which can last as long as seven months. It achieves this state of hibernation by (hopefully) building up sufficient fat stores in its body and then, once in the nest, slowing down its metabolism and lowering its body temperature in order to use as little energy as possible.

LOOK OUT FOR:

* First seen in southern Britain in the late 1980s, little egrets have spread and it is becoming increasingly common to see them inland – particu-

larly in the autumn and winter when their numbers temporarily increase due to the arrival of migrants from the continent.

* Sloes, the fruits of the blackthorn bush, are ripe now – and whenever seen in the hedgerow, are worth picking and converting into sloe gin. Traditionally made at Hallowe'en so as to be ready for drinking at Christmas, the longer you leave it before bottling, the better it becomes!

* In an exceptionally warm month (such as were the October's of 2014 and 2015), you might still see midges dancing over the surface of ditch water – and on the banks, a few butterflies still searching for nectar.

Sloes, the fruits of the blackthorn bush, are ripe now – and whenever seen in the hedgerow, are worth picking and converting into sloe gin.

NOVEMBER

Towards the end of October and into the beginning of November, hedgehogs looking for a place to hibernate can sometimes be seen; they may even be observed carrying leaves, moss or dried grass in their mouths towards the hedge bottoms and places where they intend spending the winter. In a normal year, the base of a hedgerow atop a ditch bank can prove the ideal spot but, in a particularly wet winter which causes the ditch to overflow, it is not unknown for hedgehogs to drown.

Once the temperatures drop significantly (to ten degrees centigrade or lower), it's unlikely that much in the way of insect life will be seen – nor will there be any sign of frogs, toads or grass snakes who go into a semi-dormant state at the bottom of ponds or under piles of leaves, logs or stones.

WANDERING WOODCOCK

The relative shelter afforded by a ditch bank and overhanging growth might mean that some areas of ground remain soft and friable when plac-

At the beginning of November, hedgehogs looking for a place to hibernate can sometimes be seen. (Photo: Tony Wills/ Wikimedia Commons)

es elsewhere are frozen. At such times, it's possible that birds such as woodcock, who love to probe for minute insects and grubs with their extraordinarily long beaks, will frequent the area.

Weather conditions play a predominant role in woodcock migration. In a generally mild winter, it is probable that any potential migrants will remain in their base areas abroad until a protracted spell of cold weather forces them to travel to the warmer regions of Britain. In such conditions, birds will continue to arrive long after the traditionally accepted times of late November and early December.

Many years ago, there was a common belief that woodcock only migrated on a full moon and that the majority arrived on the one that occurred nearest to Hallowe'en, but it is now generally accepted that birds will migrate throughout October, November and December, depending on the weather and wind direction.

CROUCHING WATCHER, LEAPING SALMON!

Move away from the ditch, but remain in contact with water. Depending on where you live, you may only have to shift direction towards the flowing streams and rivers in order to find arguably the most exciting seasonal thing of all.

In the rivers, the adult Atlantic salmon are migrating back to the place of their birth – the gravelly bedded waters upstream. The shallowest (but cleanest) streams and rivers can accommodate those that arrive to spawn at their final destination – and their passage is well worth watching!

LOOK OUT FOR:

* By November the wetland plants are starting to die back and appear bedraggled – but by exposing more of the bankside, other things such as moss and fungi which were hitherto hidden become more noticeable.

In the rivers the adult Atlantic salmon are migrating back to the place of their birth — the gravelly bedded waters upstream.

They are well worth looking at more closely and are an important part of the whole infrastructure of a ditch or similar waterway.

* Like woodcock, snipe can sometimes be seen probing away at the soft mud with their long beaks in search of grubs and insects. Similar in shape to woodcock, snipe are, however, half their size. Not as common as they once were, damp grass, ditches and streams are all an essential part of the snipe's habitat. As John Clare wrote in his poem, *To the Snipe*:

> Lover of swamps
> The quagmire overgrown
> With hassock tufts of sedge...
> Around thy home alone.

DECEMBER

The hedge that sometimes tops the bank to a ditch can contain a vast amount of potential life-saving food for bird life. The berries of holly, hips and hawthorn readily spring to mind but ivy is most underrated as an essential plant for both birds and insects. Its evergreen nature affords roosting for birds during cold winter nights and is also a place of semi-hibernation to insects that have survived the autumn. Ivy flowers provide a source of pollen for both the latter and winter moths, whilst the subsequent berries (which will not be fully formed until the early spring of the coming year) are taken and enjoyed by many bird varieties at a time when there is not much else about.

Birds of all description are normally sensible about what they can and cannot eat, and I have, in the past, watched with alarm whilst pheasants, in particular, have pecked away at fallen yew berries, which, as al-

It is commonly thought that yew berries are poisonous whereas in reality, it is the seeds within that are. Birds can eat berries and, provided that the seeds pass through (which they almost certainly will), suffer no consequence. (Photo: grassrootsgroundswell/ Wikimedia Commons)

most everyone knows, are deadly poisonous. In actual fact, the flesh of the berry is not, and it is only the seeds therein that are. Therefore, one can only assume that the reason pheasants and indeed all other wild birds remain unaffected after ingesting them is because the seeds pass through the body untouched.

MYSTERIOUS MISTLETOE

Mistletoe is a partly parasitic plant which utilises the period when the parent tree is bare to do its own growing and photosynthesising. In summer it is too shady for the plant to expand, so it grows leaves and sets berries in the cold season when the host tree is dormant. For this reason, it was thought to be invested with an immortal tree spirit. Such heathen attributes made sure that, unlike other evergreens such as bay and laurel, it was never likely to appear as a Christmas decoration on church premises. Occasionally, a bunch was allowed to hang in the porch, but not in the body of the church. Mistletoe has long been used in herbal medicine where it was employed for nervous disorders, internal bleeding, as a heart tonic and as an aphrodisiac. And you thought it was just for kissing beneath!

LOOK OUT FOR:

* Although mainly noticed in their breeding season, if the water is relatively clear, it is possible that you might still be able to observe a myriad of nymphs, water-beetles, water-boatmen, backswimmers, water hog-lice and even leeches – all of which overwinter in ditches. One line of thought has it that food actually becomes more available to such creatures at this time of year due to the increased oxygen content (cold water retains more oxygen) and the influx of autumnal dead leaves, on which invertebrates thrive.

* Likewise, some ponds may also contain overwintering tadpoles and, during a particularly mild December, adult amphibians might still be noticed.

* As genuinely interested though you may be, it is just possible that the opportunity to explore your own ditch and its environs might not be available. If you've not got relatively immediate access to such places, consider looking online – and joining the many and varied conservation groups which specialise in wetland regions.

* Natural history books of any description are a delight – and make the perfect Christmas present to either others or oneself. Most country-

orientated magazines carry seasonal book reviews, so take a flick through any of the field sports, smallholding and regional county 'Life' publications to find out about such books recently released onto the market.

WATCH, LEARN AND APPRECIATE

Before closing this particular chapter, it is important to reiterate what was said at the beginning. Nothing is cut-and-dried nor set in tablets of stone when it comes to nature. The 'look out for' guides outlined at the end of each month above are simply indicators of what and when you might typically discover at that time of year.

Appreciate what you find. It is easy to take for granted what might be happening both in the mini environment of a ditch and in the wider, overall view of the countryside. 'Familiarity breeds contempt' so they say – as witnessed by the eloquent writing of Richard Jefferies way back in 1880 when, in *Hodge and his Masters*, he wrote of the farm labourer as an old man.

> He had not taken much conscious note of the changing aspect of the scene around him. The violets flowered year after year... The May bloomed and scented the hedges... The green summer foliage became brown and the acorns fell from the oaks; still he laboured on, and saw the ice and snow, and heard the wind roar in the old familiar trees without much thought of it... And yet those old familiar trees, the particular hedges he had worked among..., the very turf of the meadows over which he had walked so many times... – all these things had become a part of his life.

5

DINING OUT IN A DITCH

Well, it might be stretching it a bit to say that you can dine out in a ditch but if you know what you are looking for, it is sometimes possible to find various potential ingredients to accompany the odd meal or two.

Despite being common practice for generations and championed by the likes of Richard Mabey in the early 1970s, the idea of 'food for free' has sadly been neglected of late. Nonetheless, these things go in cycles and foraging in the countryside is currently all the rage – and the ditch, whilst not as obvious a place as, say, a hedgerow, is as good a place as any to start looking. It is, however, obviously important that whatever you pick and eventually eat is correctly identified, which is why I have, in this chapter and not the others, included the Latin name against each plant described. There are many plant identification books available and the internet is a brilliant source of information – and many websites also include detailed photographs to aid recognition.

Watercress (Nasturtium officinale)
Watercress needs clear, relatively pure water in which to grow – a requirement not always found in a sluggish waterway. I have, though, frequently seen it at the confluence of gravel-bottomed streams and inlets from field drainage so it is perfectly possible that you may encounter clumps of it when out mooching.

Whilst cultivated, commercially-grown watercress can obviously be eaten raw (its peppery taste greatly enhances a summer salad), the wild variety should perhaps be treated with a little caution in areas where cows and sheep graze as it can be a host to liver fluke. Whilst a thorough washing is one way to help ensure its cleanliness, it is probably safest to cook it – the most usual way of doing so being as the main ingredient of soup.

WILD WATERCRESS SOUP
Simple and easy, all that is required for four people is:

Fresh watercress – a good handful per person

2 large potatoes

Knob of butter (more precisely 'measured' as a heaped tablespoon!)

Glug of olive oil (Some cooks define a 'glug' as being when you would hear the bottle 'glug' back at you when pouring fast – others say 2–3 tablespoons!)

A stock cube (chicken or vegetable) dissolved in boiling water as per the packet's instructions

Salt and freshly ground pepper to taste

4 tablespoons of single cream

Peel and cube the potatoes and cook them gently in the oil and butter until they are starting to soften. Add the dissolved stock cube and simmer for about 10 minutes – whilst doing so, roughly chop the watercress and then add it to the potato/stock mix before cooking for a further 5 minutes or so (there's very little precision needed in soup-making!). Stir occasionally and then liquidise. Allow the soup to cool a little before adding salt and pepper, and finally the cream.

NB: Whilst normally served warm, Wild Watercress Soup is equally tasty served cold as a summer soup.

Yarrow (Achillea millefolium)

Young yarrow leaves can be added to a salad or stirred into a green salsa with olive oil and lemon. The older fronds are, however, best cooked. Start by stripping the leaves from the stalks; rinse them well before putting them in a pan with a drop or two of water and a little salt. Cover and heat (shaking the pan to prevent burning) until tender and then either add them to mashed potato or coat with a cheese sauce.

Chickweed (Stellaria media)

Chickweed can be found in many parts of the countryside – including the areas around a ditch. Use the washed leaves as a component of a green salad containing such things as rocket and watercress (*see above with regard to the safe use of wild watercress*): the peppery taste of the latter combines beautifully with the sweeter taste of the chickweed.

To use chickweed cooked, the whole plant should be harvested and the roots removed. Rinse and cook in a covered pan (*as with yarrow above*) until it wilts. Drain and dry before either incorporating it into mashed potato or topping it with grated cheese and placing it under the grill just until the cheese begins to melt.

NB: Whilst a 'weed', conservationists might nevertheless be alarmed at the amount of chickweed required for cooking – two tight handfuls will only produce roughly a tablespoon – but no-one is suggesting that you denude your local area of the stuff; rather that it's worth trying as a one-off seasonal treat.

HOW NOT TO FALL FOUL OF THE LAW

Under the *Wildlife and Countryside Act* of 1981, many native species of plants are offered at least some protection. Technically, it is illegal to uproot any wild plant without permission from the landowner or occupier ('uproot' being defined as to 'dig up or otherwise remove the plant from the land on which it is growing', whether or not it actually has roots; and, for the purposes of the legislation, the term 'plant' also includes algae, lichens and fungi).

Some plants are more protected than others. The Act includes a schedule of endangered plants protected against intentional picking, uprooting and destruction (unless a licence is obtained from the relevant authority, or the damage is a result of a lawful activity and could not reasonably have been avoided). This schedule (Schedule 8) is revised every five years and the latest updates can be found by looking online at: *http://jncc.defra.gov.uk/page-4341*

The website provides guidance for people who wish to pick plants for pleasure, pursue botanical studies, collect specimens for educational purposes or gather wild food for individual or family use – and allows that picking is acceptable in some circumstances. As a general rule, though:

* Only pick flowers and foliage from large patches of the plant.
* Always pick in moderation.
* Take care not to damage other vegetation unintentionally.

Bladder Campion (*Silene vulgaris*)

Bladder campion, so-named because of the bladder-like calyx (a bulge made up of fused sepals) just behind the flowers, is found in many rural areas, including the banks of some ditches. Despite its somewhat unattractive-sounding moniker, bladder campion can be used to make a sauce for tagliatelle pasta – and does, in fact, appear in a classic recipe cooked in the San Marino region of Italy.

Bladder Campion Pasta Sauce

300 g bladder campion
600 g tomato sauce
50 g bacon, chopped
1 garlic clove, chopped
1 onion, chopped
120 ml dry white wine
Olive oil
Sea salt to taste

Heat a little olive oil in a pan then add the bacon, garlic and onion. Fry for about 5 minutes or until softened, then add the white wine. Bring to a boil and continue cooking until almost all the wine has evaporated. At this point add the campion and the tomato sauce. Return to the heat, season to taste with salt then reduce to a simmer and cook for about 12 minutes.

In the meantime, bring a pan of salted water to a boil, add the tagliatelle and cook for about 4 minutes, or until al dente. Drain then add to the pan with the sauce and stir in well. Turn into a bowl and, for that authentic Italian taste, serve accompanied by grated Parmesan cheese.

Bog Myrtle (Myrica gale)

Bog myrtle sounds almost as unattractive as bladder campion but, as with that particular plant, names can be deceptive and bog myrtle has long been used in the flavouring of drinks – not least of which was the 'weak beer' produced in Anglo-Saxon times.

Not found universally throughout the British Isles (possibly because of the fact that, over the centuries, some of its natural habitat has been drained and become unattractive), the plant is, however, what biologists refer to as being 'locally common' in that it thrives in parts of the country that contain damp, acid areas such as the ditches and streams of North Wales and the moorlands of England and Scotland.

Should you find bog myrtle in your region, try using the leaves to flavour a cocktail-type drink or, as is recommended in some foraging books, as an ingredient in chicken stuffing.

Golden Saxifrage (Chrysosplenium oppositifolium)

A known lover of damp, shady places, golden saxifrage is most often found along the sides of ditches and streams that run through woodland areas.

It also thrives in boggy ground. Recognised by its yellow flowers in March and April, it is, however, the small, succulent leaves that are of interest to the foraging frequenter of ditches. Use them in a salad – ideally with other leaves that have been harvested from nature.

Wild Garlic *(Allium ursinum)*

Like the golden saxifrage, wild garlic is at its best in late spring and, at that time of year, can easily be identified by its thick, broad leaves and small white flowers clustered at the end of a long stem. Each plant can have up to 20 leaves sprouting from a single stalk and if you rub any part of the plant between finger and thumb, there will be an easily recognisable garlic smell – in fact, where wild garlic grows in profusion, there's no need to touch it at all as the air is full of its not unpleasant but definitely pungent smell. Thriving as it does in damp, shady areas, there is every chance that you will come across wild garlic as you explore the ditches and streams of Britain – particularly in the south-west.

A fossilised impression of a wild garlic leaf was found at a Mesolithic (10,000–7,000 BC) settlement in Denmark, proving it to be one of man's oldest foods. A plant known and used for centuries in many European countries, you could do worse than experience its culinary delights in an asparagus and garlic risotto.

ASPARAGUS AND WILD GARLIC RISOTTO

200 g Carnaroli risotto rice
1 bunch fresh local asparagus
75 g butter
150 ml white wine
Vegetable stock, hot
3 finely diced shallots
12 leaves wild garlic
1 dessertspoon acid butter (see below)
100 g parmesan, grated
Salt and pepper

Acid butter
1 shallot, sliced
100 ml white wine
75 ml white wine vinegar
1 tablespoon double cream
375 g butter, cold

To make the acid butter, place the sliced shallot, white wine and vinegar in a pan and reduce. Once reduced, add cream. Then, over a low heat, slowly stir in the cold butter until it is all incorporated together in the pan. Pass through a strainer into a plastic container with an air-tight lid and put in the fridge. If this is kept in the fridge, it will last a month.

To make the risotto, trim the leaves from the asparagus and remove the bottom inch or so that is hard and pale. Slice the main part of the spears but leave the top 2 inches whole. Blanch the spears and slices separately in salted boiling water and refresh in iced water.

Finely dice the shallots and melt the butter in a heavy-bottomed pan before adding the shallots and sweating until translucent. Add the rice and cool for 2 minutes, always stirring. Add the wine and keep stirring until it is all absorbed. Slowly incorporate the hot stock a little at a time. Keep stirring! (It is important to keep stirring as the stock is being absorbed in order to release the starch from the grains, making the risotto creamier.) After 15–17 minutes the rice should be cooked and have the texture of a peanut. Add the grated parmesan and the sliced asparagus, keeping the spears for garnish. Add the acid butter and stir in well. At the last possible minute, finely cut the wild garlic and add to the risotto. Garnish with asparagus spears and wild garlic flowers.

NB: There are, of course, many variations on a theme – as evidenced by the wild garlic, mushroom and green bean risotto illustrated.

Wild garlic, mushroom and green bean risotto. (Photo: courtesy of Philip Watts)

Common Nettle (Urtica dioica)

Most usually referred to as a stinging nettle, the common nettle is just that – common! It can be found almost anywhere and everywhere, including the banks of ditches where the build-up of nutrients deposited over years of seasonal water level fluctuations provides an ideal growing medium. Although not strictly relevant, it is of interest to note that wherever you see a good crop of stinging nettles, the soil below is likely to be good quality – and if a clump grows in the garden of a newly-purchased house, that's the place to dig your vegetable patch. The nettles will require continual weeding for a year or two, but the results with your nitrogen-loving vegetables will be worth the effort.

Very much underrated as a natural food source, nettles contain a surprising amount of protein and the young shoots can be nipped out and wilted in much the same way as one would spinach. The leaves also make a pleasant-tasting tea, and many of the old gardeners made a nettle-based liquid fertiliser for use on their crops.

Goosegrass *(Galium aparine)*

Where it grows in abundance you sometimes don't need to go looking for and harvesting goosegrass as it will quite readily find you and attach itself to your clothing! Also known as 'cleavers', the plant grows under hedges, in wayside verges and on the banks of ditches and streams. Harsh to the touch because of the many backward-facing hooks that help it cling on to other vegetation (and your clothes!), once plunged into boiling water or steamed, they soften and become quite palatable. Alternatively, pick the springtime shoot tips and include them in a stew or add them when making home-made soup.

THE NETTLE-EATING CHAMPIONSHIPS!

Best cooked in order to rid it of its hypodermic, histamine-injecting hairs, there are, however, those amongst us who revel in eating nettles raw!

At Marsham, in Dorset, every June some 50 challengers are each given 60 cm (2 ft) stalks of nettles and have an hour to chew through as many as possible – the winner being the person with the longest length of empty stalk.

It all started as a contest between two farmers as to which had the longest nettles. One of the contestants, a certain Alex Williams, produced one around 15 ft in length and declared that if anyone had a longer one he would eat his – well, wouldn't you just know it, someone had and Alex was forced to honour his promise; thus beginning the annual nettle-eating contest.

Fennel *(Foeniculum vulgare)*

In parts of France, I've found wild fennel growing in abundance – and regularly used it as a flavouring for fish dishes. Easily recognised by its frond-like leaves, mustard-yellow flowers and distinctive-smelling strong stem, fennel has been in vogue for both culinary and medicinal purposes throughout Europe since at least Roman times. Unusual in that it likes both the type of environment typically found on the quiet roadside verge and also damp places, there will almost certainly be ditch banks in Britain where specimens thrive.

A FISHY BUSINESS!

There are, in some small streams and particularly clean, generally fast-flowing ditches, freshwater mussels – some of which are technically safe to eat. However, bearing in mind the possibilities of potential stomach upsets (or worse), tempting though it may be to try foraging and eating such things, one really ought to err on the side of caution.

Due to their burrowing habits, freshwater mussels frequently end up storing degrees of pollution in their soft tissue – and eating mussels contaminated with toxins can make you ill. Having said that, the danger of eating contaminated mussels also exists in saltwater mussels so all risks are relative.

Some foragers, eager to make full use of what nature has to offer, say that provided you 'purge' your freshwater mussels by keeping them for a few days in frequently changed clean water (in a fish tank perhaps), all should be well. Those who have tried it do, however, admit that the resultant feast is nowhere near as tasty as the saltwater variety bought from the fishmongers!

NB: With mussels; irrespective of whether they are salt or freshwater varieties, only cook the closed ones – and only eat the ones that are open after cooking!

As well as using its fine, threadlike leaves fresh on fish, they can be cut and hung to dry for use out of season. The seeds of fennel are also of value to the cook and are best harvested in late autumn, dried in a cool oven and stored in air-tight jars.

Many herbs found out in the countryside – including wild fennel – are a tasty addition to stuffed jacket potatoes. (Photo: courtesy of Philip Watts)

Meadowsweet
(Filipendula ulmaria)

Meadowsweet is a perennial herb, growing in damp meadows, ditches and bogs, at the edges of ponds, on riverbanks and in damp open woodland. It can also be used to make a very attractive-sounding combination of panna cotta and sorbet by including blackberries foraged from the hedgerow.

MEADOWSWEET PANNA COTTA AND BLACKBERRY SORBET

To make the panna cotta:

3 leaves of gelatine

250 ml milk

250 ml double cream

25 g sugar

1 good handful of meadowsweet flowers

For the sorbet:

300 g caster sugar

300 ml water

400 g hedgerow-harvested, thoroughly-washed blackberries

Soak the gelatine leaves in cold water until soft. In the meanwhile, in a pan, simmer together the milk, cream, sugar and meadowsweet flowers. Once sufficiently infused, remove the flowers and discard. Gently squeeze the gelatine to remove the water and add it to the pan contents. Take off the heat and stir until dissolved. Pour into ramekins then refrigerate for at least an hour.

In a pan, simmer together the caster sugar and water to make a syrup. Allow to cool before adding the blackberries and blending in a food processor. Cover and chill for 2 hours.

Sweet Cicely (Myrrhis odorata)

Given the first part of its Latin name, I did wonder whether sweet cicely was related to the plant that gave the oil extract brought by one of the Three Wise Men to baby Jesus – but apparently not! Its leaves are, though, quite sweet tasting (and have an aniseed fragrance) and as such, can be used as a flavouring for stewed fruits. This natural sweetness makes sweet cicely a useful addition to any culinary situation where sugar needs to be added as, according to the experts, it helps to save almost half the sugar that would otherwise be needed. Useful information for diabetics or those on a diet!

> **A TUFT OF MEADOWSWEET**
>
> Meadowsweet has even attracted the attention of at least one poet – as can be seen in the first verse of this poem by George Barlow (1847-1913):
>
> A tuft of withered meadow-sweet,
> Just that and nothing more:
> And yet what hosts of memories fleet
> The dry old fronds restore!
> A tuft of withered meadow-sweet,
> No gaudy pink or rose;
> And yet the dried-up leaves I see,
> Long scorned of butterfly and bee,
> Are holier, dearer, unto me
> Than any flower that blows –
> Than any flower that blows, my love,
> Than any flower that blows!

In his book *Food for Free*, Richard Mabey rates the plant highly and mentions that the 16th century herbalist John Gerard was also a fan. Gerard recommended the roots eaten after boiling and the leaves as part of a salad. It was, though, the seeds that really got this particular herbalist's taste-buds going:

> ... eaten as a salad whilest they are yet greene, with oyle, vinegar and pepper, they exceed all other sallads by many degrees, both in pleasantness of taste, sweetness of smell, and wholesomeness for the cold and feeble stomack.

The leaves of sweet cicely are sweet tasting and can be used to flavour stewed fruits amongst other things. (Photo: H. Zell/ Wikimedia Commons)

In modern jargon, what's not to like?!

Water Mint (*Mentha aquatica*)

Most meals are best finished with a cup of coffee, or cup of tea – and a herbal tea that might cost you a couple of pounds or more per cup in a restaurant can be had for free from the banks of a ditch, stream or similar rural waterway! Whilst there are several types of wild mint to be found in the British countryside (all of which can be identified by their easily recognisable leaves and obviously minty smell), the water mint variety is arguably the commonest.

As with all mint, whether it be garden-grown or wild, water mint can be used fresh to make mint sauce to accompany lamb, dried for later use, mixed into couscous, used as an ingredient of some chutneys and, of course, as a refreshing tea – said by some to settle an upset stomach.

A few leaves in a mug and covered with boiling water will do, but better results can be obtained by the following method:

(Mint) Tea for Two!

After washing the stems and leaves of four or five mint sprigs, place them in a cafetière and top up with boiling water. Replace the lid and plunger, but do not 'plunge' until the mint has had a chance to infuse (about 3 minutes). Then plunge gently, pour and drink.

THE DOWN-SIDE OF FORAGING

But, before you go out full of enthusiasm, armed with stick, basket, penknife and plant identification notes, it is as well to think of the possible negative aspects of foraging. As writer, author and broadcaster Jay Raynor said in an *Observer* article of September 10, 2014, 'just because you can go foraging doesn't mean you should'.

Although an individual picking the leaves of a few plants is unlikely to affect the ecology of the countryside, if everyone rushed out there and did the same then things might be different. In practice this is unlikely but more and more articles are appearing in the mainstream press about 'irresponsible' or more often 'criminal' foragers. Apparently, if you can believe what you read, 'gangs' are 'pillaging' our countryside.

Warnings are issued each year over the possible harm done to the ecosystem of places such as the New Forest, Epping Forest and Ashdown Forest. Some feel that damage has already been done. As one blog-writer puts it: 'Too many of the leather-hatted professional foragers have become enemies of the countryside, rather than its custodians.'

Jay Raynor, in his *Observer* article, looked at the current trend for foraging in a very different way, saying that the biggest argument against it 'is the lacklustre and uninspiring food that so often results from all that clomping about... Too many [foragers] end up chirping about how one foraged ingredient tastes of lemon and another of liquorice and a third of aniseed.' To which comments Mr Raynor says he wants to shout: 'so why don't you leave the poor bloody wild plants alone and just use lemon, liquorice and aniseed instead?'

Whilst he may well have a point, it would be a shame if one didn't occasionally gather and bring home to use some of what you might discover when mooching about in the environs of a ditch – just as it would be if you didn't consider or even know about some of the more obscure sporting and leisure activities performed in, around and over ditches. To find out more, read on!

⑥

THE GAMES PEOPLE PLAY

Whilst ditches and similar waterways are undoubtedly crucial in taking away surplus water, preventing flooding and as a valuable ecosystem and habitat for plants and wildlife, it is, however, important not to become too bogged down (pun intended!) with the serious side of a year spent in and around a ditch. There are several events throughout Britain and Europe where less environmentally sensitive, or even specially constructed, lengths of ditches are used for the purpose of competition, tradition and amusement – the last usually being more on the part of the spectators rather than the competitors!

BOG-SNORKELLING

Allegedly originating in Llanwrtyd Wells, Wales, in 1975, bog-snorkelling is nowadays also practised in several other countries. Nonetheless, Llanwrtyd Wells is still the home of the World Bog Snorkelling Championships held in August each year. Contestants have to complete two consecutive lengths of a 55 metre (180 ft) water-filled ditch cut through a peat bog in the shortest time possible using snorkel and flippers and no recognised swimming stroke. They also need to keep their heads underwater whilst doing so – except for the occasional glance in search of direction!

Bog-snorkelling adds a whole new meaning to the title of this book! (Photo: image by Fotograferen.net/author; Rud-gr/Wikimedia Commons)

As with ditch-jumping (see below), bog-snorkelling is likely to be a far more enjoyable occasion for the spectators than it ever is for the competitors although, unlike ditch-jumping where the most proficient at least have a chance of remaining dry, anyone choosing to indulge in bog-snorkelling knows from the outset that they are going to get cold, wet and muddy. Why then, at the last championships, there were eager participants from France, Germany, Belgium, Por-

ON YER BIKE!
At the same venue of the bog-snorkelling championships, the World Mountain Bike Bog Snorkelling Championships take place (no, really, I'm not making it up…). Apparently competitors must cycle along a length of deep ditch on a special lead-weighted bike wearing a weighted backpack. It's events like this that make Britain great!

tugal, Sweden, Eire, South Africa, Australia, New Zealand, the USA, Hong Kong and Mali, as well as from Britain, is anybody's guess!

DITCH-JUMPING

Undoubtedly somewhat remiss of me, but in my book *Curious Country Customs* (David & Charles, 2007) I neglected to mention the ancient sport of ditch-jumping as it is done in Britain! Known in most of Europe as 'fierljeppen' (wide-ditch vaulting), ditch-jumping seemingly originated in Holland and was first brought over to the fenlands of East Anglia. Although nowadays mainly an amusing spectator sport – there are always those who like to see a participant end up in the water – it does, nevertheless, have a serious and competitive element and the best of them all are able to vault distances of over 21 metres (a 2011 World Record set by Bart Helmholt). Originally, though, being able to pole-vault the farmland ditches and dykes had a purely practical purpose as it enabled herdsmen to get about their land in order to check livestock without getting their feet wet, or a need for a bridge.

Like all games, ditch-jumping has its rules and techniques. According to one website: 'A flexible pole [nowadays made of carbon] is set upright in the stretch of water to be jumped. A jump consists of an intense sprint to the pole, jumping and grabbing it, climbing to the top of the pole to gain ultimate distance whilst at the same time trying to control the forward and lateral movements over the stretch of water to be jumped, the intention of the jump is to finish with a graceful landing on a sand bed on the opposite bank to the start.'

Although nowadays mainly an amusing spectator sport – there are always those who like to see a participant end up in the water – 'fierljeppen' or wide-ditch jumping has a serious and competitive element. (Photo: Peter van der Sluijis/Wikimedia Commons)

Whilst there is no age limit, any competitors must, however, 'be at an age when they have developed full upper body strength', normally 16 or 18 years. The most successful jumpers tend to be aged between 25 and 35 years and, because of all the diverse skills required to be a dyke-jumper, 'are considered to be very complete athletes, with superbly developed strength and co-ordination'. As to its attraction as a spectator sport – as well as the obvious possibility of competitors ending up totally submerged in the muddy water, vaulting poles can fall in the wrong direction, jumpers can leap at the wrong moment and a mistimed grip can leave even the best of 'fierljeppers' sliding down into the ditch.

NUTS CHALLENGE

Most of us as children fixed a rope from a tree and swung on it over a stream or muddy ditch. The consequences were almost inevitable – indeed television programmes such as *You've Been Framed* frequently feature amateur clips of those who have attempted such activities only to end up totally immersed in the mud and/or water.

Some take these childhood experiences to a higher level in adult life and at a venue near Dorking, Surrey, the annual Nuts Challenge has been held for almost two decades. At its inception, an assault course was built and comprised the obligatory rope swing over a muddy ditch and the types of obstacles one might find on the average army training ground.

Over the ensuing years, however, much more has been added and the course is nowadays some seven kilometres in length, containing wooden structures, climbing nets and precarious-looking floating platforms. In addition to the man-made parts of the course, the natural topography is such that contestants spend much of their time jumping in and climbing out of slippery-sided river beds, climbing hills and wading through thick mud.

For most, one lap of this extremely tough course would be enough but there are those incredibly fit (and fool-hardy!) athletes who choose to undertake up to four laps (a total of 28 kilometres) of the circuit. Accepted as being one of the toughest events of its type, many of the competitors take part in order to raise money for charity so whether or not they finish the course (and well over half of the people in the longer options do not), it is, they feel, well worth attempting what is reckoned to be one of Britain's best obstacle events.

HORSES FOR (WATER)COURSES

Some of the equestrian jumps seen on a cross-country course which incorporates a ditch/bank/fence combination owe their existence to obstacles originally found when out fox-hunting. The 'Normandy' bank is one where the ditch precedes the bank and a 'coffin' is one where water

YOU CAN TAKE A DOG TO WATER...

Many a gundog trainer has been seen paddling about in a ditch with their young dogs in order to accustom them to water. It is extremely important not to over-face a puppy in the early stages, and a ditch or similar shallow watercourse is the perfect place for a dog to learn how to deal with water-based obstacles once they are taken out into the fields and woodlands on a shooting day. A ditch is also the perfect place to teach a dog to jump from bank to bank – and to retrieve from over a stretch of water. Some gundog owners also enjoy competing with their dogs at working tests and field trials, where the tests are deliberately laid out so as to include rough ground, fences and ditches.

Great care must, however, be taken not to use natural ditches at such times of the year when reptiles and small animals may be breeding and ground-nesting birds either sitting on eggs or brooding recently-hatched chicks.

lies at the bottom of a bank on both sides. A 'ditch' in cross-country is nowadays a dry one – but very wide (sometimes as much as almost 12 feet/3.5 metres). Perhaps most interesting, though, is the one known by the horse fraternity as a 'trakehner' – apparently originating from the Trakehnen region of East Prussia which was, before being drained by the Prussian kings in the 17th and 18th centuries, wetland. A trakehner was, then, originally a fence line constructed at the bottom of a drainage ditch rather than, as might be expected, on either side. According to *Wikipedia*, this ditch/fence combination was used by the stud farm (established in 1732) which produced the Trakehner breed of horse, as a test for a young horses' suitability for breeding and war mounts.

HARE PIE SCRAMBLE AND BOTTLE KICKING

On Easter Monday, the people of Hallaton in Lincolnshire continue a custom which has its origins in the mid-18th century. Traditionally a hare pie was first eaten and its remains were taken to Hare Pie Hill where they were then spread on the ground – possibly as some kind of fertility ritual stemming from the Dark Age when a hare would regularly be sacrificed at this time of year in honour of the goddess Eostre. In fact, in 1790, the vicar of Hallaton attempted to ban the event because of its non-Christian beginnings but was forced to back down when the threatening graffiti message 'No pie, no parson' mysteriously appeared on the wall of his home.

More applicable to this particular chapter, however, is the fact that a 'bottle-kicking' contest was – and still is – incorporated into the occasion. Facing each other, two teams made up of villagers from the neighbouring villages of Hallaton and Medbourne compete over possession of three ribbon-bedecked barrels ('bottles'). During the next few hours every effort is made to either roll or carry them to their own particular village boundary streams situated a mile apart. To do so, the contestants have to negotiate hedges, lanes, barbed wire fences and several muddy ditches. There are no rules to the game – which might perhaps be better described as a free-for-all – and at the end of the day, a scorer announces the winners who are then chaired to the town cross where the real festivities begin in earnest, commencing with both teams sharing the beer contained within the final 'bottle'.

KAYAKING EX-STREAMS!

Obviously somewhat larger than the average ditch in the British Isles, drainage ditches in British Columbia are seemingly the place to 'enjoy' some madcap kayaking exploits. Whilst it's necessary to carry one's kayak upstream, once it's launched it is apparently possible for kayaking experts to reach speeds of between 35 and 45 miles per hour on the downward journey!

Things are, though, somewhat more sedate in Hawaii, where the less experienced kayaker can book themselves in for a trip down 100-year-old ditches which were originally created to carry rain water down to the lower lands for agricultural usage. The speed of the kayak stays pretty constant at around four or five miles per hour, and is propelled by the current of water as it travels downstream rather than the efforts of a frantically paddling oarsman.

SWAMP SOCCER

Not quite a muddy ditch but the principle is the same: get down and dirty – and very wet! Apparently the 'sport' of swamp soccer originated in Finland where it was initially used as a training activity for soldiers and athletes – the idea being that playing silly beggars in such conditions is physically challenging and helps boost physical strength. I'm certainly not going to challenge the veracity of the claim, but nor will I be participating in the sport anytime soon!

BEATING THE BOUNDS

Not so much a game as a legitimate opportunity to give a child a good thrashing, the ancient British custom of 'beating the bounds' quite often involved streams and ditches!

Many moons ago, it was considered imperative that village youngsters learned the parish boundaries at a very early age and so, either during 'Rogation' week or on Ascension Day, as part of the annual Christian ceremonies, they were taken round the various landmarks that denoted the boundaries. These could have included specific stones, ancient trees, hedge lines – and ditches. During the 1800s, publisher William Hone produced an annual *Year Book of Daily Recreation and Information*, in one of which a certain William Barnes contributed this piece explaining how the tradition was carried out in Dorset during his childhood:

> A Perambulation, or, as it might be more correctly called, a circumambulation, is the custom of going round the boundaries of a manor or parish, with witnesses, to determine and preserve recollection of its extent, and to see that no encroachments have been made upon it, and that the landmarks have not been taken away. It is a proceeding commonly regulated by the steward, who takes with him a few men and several boys who are required to particularly observe the boundaries traced out, and thereby qualify themselves for witnesses in the event of any dispute about the landmarks or extent of the manor at a future day. In order that they may not forget the lines and marks of separation they take pains at almost every turning. For instance, if the boundary be a stream, one of the boys is tossed into it; if a broad ditch, the boys are offered money to jump over it, in which they, of course, fail, and pitch into the mud, where they stick as firmly as if they had been rooted there for the season; if a hedge, a sapling is cut out of it and used in afflicting that part of their bodies upon which they rest in the posture between standing and lying; if a wall, they are to have a race on the top of it, when, in trying to pass each other, they fall over on each side, some descending, perhaps, into the still stygian waters of a ditch, and others thrusting the 'human face divine' into a bed of nettles; if the boundary be a sunny bank, they sit down upon it and get a treat of beer and bread and cheese, and, perhaps, a glass of spirits.

A-MAZING

According to widely held belief, a Winchester scholar of the late 1600s, for some reason unable to indulge in the more usual sort of games with his fellows during a school holiday, set about creating a 'miz-maze' on nearby St Catherine's Hill. A miz-maze is more usually made of cut turf which forms the maze itself, but the one which can still be seen on the hill above Winchester is one of only two such historic mazes (the other being at Saffron Walden, Essex) whereby the maze is created by shallow channels or ditches. It is even more unusual in that, whereas many mazes are circular, the one on St Catherine's Hill is roughly square-shaped.

In his 1922 book *Mazes and Labyrinths*, W. H. Matthews remarked that 'The interest of this maze lies not so much in the fanciful ascription of its origin as in the fact that it has apparently been cut, or re-cut, by somebody who did not understand the meaning of the plan given him to work upon' and that the maze being formed by the channels or ditches rather than the turf dug from the ground 'is hardly likely to have been the case in the original design'.

No matter what the unknown Winchester schoolboy's original plan, the fact remains that, by the middle of the 1800s, the miz-maze had become weather-worn and almost erased and so, according to Matthews, 'was re-cut by the Warden of Winchester, who was guided by a plan in

The miz-maze at St Catherine's Hill, Hampshire.

the possession of a lady residing in the neighbourhood [and] possibly the misinterpretation of the plan occurred on this occasion'.

Owned by Winchester College, St Catherine's Hill and the miz-maze make for perfect genteel entertainment on a warm summer's afternoon – once you've climbed up the quite steep incline, that is!

METAL DETECTING IN THE MUD

The banks and immediate environment on the edges of ditches and small inland waterways might well be the ideal place to spend time with a metal detector because, through the years, flooding and general water movement is quite likely to have deposited metallic items of interest from upstream into the silt or soil.

Whilst little harm may be done with a little judicious digging, great care must be taken when contemplating running a detector over other kinds of ditches and dykes, many of which may be historically ancient. It is, in fact, illegal to randomly metal detect in places of archaeological interest unless under licence. In late 2014, treasure hunters using metal detectors were suspected of being responsible for as many as 50 holes which mysteriously appeared on the ridge-line between Perseverance Hill and Black Hill in the Malvern Hills. A local newspaper also reported that similar irresponsible digging threatened the Shire Ditch, 'an important archaeological site, which runs along the spine of the Malvern Hills... The ditch, which has historically marked the boundary between Herefordshire and Worcestershire, is thought to date back to the Bronze Age, and... is designated as a Scheduled Monument, which means that it is an offence to destroy or damage it, or to use a metal detector there.'

Even on less important agricultural land, metal detecting may be restricted or prohibited under the conditions of one of the Countryside Stewardship Schemes. With that in mind, should you be tempted to spend what would no doubt be an enjoyable hour or more combing the ditch banks and silted areas in search of interesting objects, it is undoubtedly advisable to first of all seek permission from the landowner.

POOHSTICKS

Definitely far less telling on the participant than any other game, sport or tradition I've previously mentioned is the pleasant occupation of

'Poohsticks', and I'd like to think that there isn't a person alive who hasn't played the game at some point in their childhood. A sluggish ditch is not, I must admit, necessarily the best place to indulge in such a pastime but, in places where a stretch of water runs relatively fast and there are not too many curves and bends – and there is a footbridge of some description across it – it's as good a way as any to while away the odd five minutes or so!

Invented, of course, by Winnie the Pooh (at least according to his creator A. A. Milne in his classic, *The House at Pooh Corner*), the rules are simple and involve two or more competitors doing nothing more arduous than selecting identifiable short lengths of sticks and throwing them upstream of the bridge before then watching whose is the first to be carried by the current under the bridge and out on the other side. According to the story, the game occurred by accident rather than design and as a result of Pooh unintentionally dropping a fir cone into the water. Sticks were eventually substituted in place of fir cones as individual sticks were apparently easier to recognise than fir cones.

As picturesque a place as any for a game of Poohsticks!

FUTURE YEARS

Whilst people may play games, forage for naturally occurring food, explore on a monthly basis and learn much about wildlife from time spent in and around a ditch, ditches and other similar waterways serve a serious purpose. Constructed principally to drain the land and send surplus water seawards via streams and rivers, the efficiency or otherwise of such man-made channels has been brought to the fore due to the catastrophic flooding of recent winters. While there are obviously many other contributory reasons, when it comes to the value of the seemingly inconsequential ditch, there are undoubted lessons to be learned for the future. However, before one can go forward, it is sometimes necessary to look back and history needs to be heeded.

Draining and allowing water to get away to the sea with a minimum impact on the land through which it travels is generally seen as being a 'good thing'. Sometimes, though, doing so can have unexpected consequences, as the parliaments of the mid-1700s discovered when, after almost a century of battling with the fen-man of eastern England intent on preventing the draining of the fenland, they were successful in doing so. As the land dried, it shrunk and affected the water table... and became more prone to flooding. Pumping stations, powered initially by windmills and subsequently steam and diesel-driven engines, were needed to control the levels.

Despite what might have been previously mentioned elsewhere in these pages, the inhabitants of the Netherlands – well known for their innovative drainage methods – have not always got it right either. Despite their knowledge and tenacity in, King Canute-like, keeping water from their door, there have been unexpected traumas over the years – not least of which were the storms of 1953 which meant that the defences were broken (it would have taken far more than the well-known Dutch boy sticking his finger in the dam) and 1,800 people died.

This tragedy did, though, ensure that much more was done and further, far more revolutionary plans were put into being, not least of

Holland's network of sluices, locks, dykes and dams have been described as being one of the 'Seven Wonders of the Modern World'.

which was the 'Delta Works', a network of sluices, locks, dykes and dams that the American Society of Civil Engineers went on to describe as being one of the 'Seven Wonders of the Modern World'.

Whilst there are undoubtedly lessons to be learned as a result of Dutch experience and know-how, it is not just a question of how best to avoid

THE BOY WITH HIS FINGER IN THE DYKE

For those who are not aware of the story – which although set in Holland was actually written by American writer Mary Maples-Dodge in her 1865 book, *Hans Brinker; or, the Silver Skates: a story of life in Holland* – it recounts the time when, on his way to school, a Dutch boy noticed a leak in one of the numerous dykes built to prevent flooding and control water passage and stuck his finger in the hole in order to stem the flow. Eventually the boy was noticed by a passer-by who dashed off to fetch tools and assistance and the leak was sealed.

A little like the proverbs, 'a stitch in time saves nine' and 'for the sake of a nail, a shoe was lost… for the sake of a shoe, a horse was lost… for the sake of a horse, the battle was lost', the tale is told to illustrate the fact that if people act quickly and in time, potential disaster can often be averted. Can anything be more appropriate to include in this particular chapter?!

flooding issues in the future; there is the on-going maintenance of Britain's ditches and other watercourses to consider. As Angus Collingwood-Cameron of the Northern Farmers and Landowners Group phrased it so succinctly in a letter to *The Field* in July 2014:

'I can only hope that the one positive result of last winter's floods will be a rethink on the management of our precious riparian resources, with a shift in emphasis from the Clip-Board Conservationists back to those with a day-to-day knowledge of our rivers, operating within a sensible, regulatory framework.'

IN THE MEDIA

In June 2014, a parliamentary sub-committee of MPs got together to discuss the ramifications of the previous winter's flooding on the Somerset Levels – and deduced that nothing of any consequence could be achieved without more dredging which does, of course, cost money. More finance was promised but it remains to be seen whether or not that promise – and the on-going work currently being overseen by the Environment Agency – is sufficient. Somewhat ironically, later the same month, BBC Radio 4's *Farming Today* programme contained a piece saying that the deadline for applying for emergency funding for farmers was rapidly approaching and that, at the time, of the £10 million made available by the government, less than 20 per cent of that figure had been allocated. According to various interviewees, the reason why not more farmers had applied was because the necessary form-filling had been made far too complicated – and that the various cut-off points of the grant's availability were not practical. Immediate damage can obviously be identified but more long-term effects of the flooding might not materialise until several months afterwards – by which time the money put aside would apparently have been returned to its original 'pot' destined for general farming and forestry projects.

WHO PAYS?

In the Netherlands there is, by law, an inspection of waterways (particularly dykes) every five years. In addition, there is a vast body of locally-based water-related agencies responsible for flood protection – each of which make an annual financial demand on local residents in order to keep them safe.

After the 2014 flooding in south-west England, and that of the winter of 2015/16 in northern England – disasters which, unlike Holland in the 1950s, did not, thankfully, leave anyone dead but nevertheless an allegedly disputed number of rural residents without homes and farmers without the wherewithal to immediately carry on (thank goodness both for the 'Fodder Aid' scheme originally set up in late 2013 by East Anglian farmer Andrew Ward and for individual farmers in areas unaffected by the flooding who 'fostered' livestock in the interim – actions which alleviated the immediate problem), inhabitants were asked by the media whether they would be prepared to shoulder such costs if demanded by subsequent legislation. Whilst the farmers were prepared to pay, it seemed that, from a 'vox-pop', the vast majority of householders were not and, like the proverbial ostrich, stuck their heads in the sand or, perhaps more appropriately in this instance, the sand-bag.

Funding at local and national level

In November 2014, county councillors approved plans to form a new flood prevention body in Somerset, the purpose being to 'reduce the likelihood, duration and impact of flooding in the county'. The new organisation, known as the Somerset Rivers Authority (SRA), is an important part of the 20-year Flood Action Plan, which was prepared after the extreme floods at the government's request. Funding is obviously a crucial issue and, at the time of writing, *all* organisations involved in the Flood Action Plan are urging a clear-cut commitment from the government to give the

The money to replace and strengthen damaged banks – and prevent further flooding in the future – comes from a variety of sources, much of it local.

£2.7 million of funding needed in order to get a 'Shadow' Somerset Rivers Authority up and running in 2015. The SRA's proposed plan is then to raise funds locally through a countywide charge from 2016. As Somerset County Council leader John Osman said at the time: 'Unless we receive interim funding… all of the good work which we have achieved over the past nine months will count for very little.'

FRACKING

Are our humble ditches and dykes likely to be affected by the process of fracking in future years? According to some, it seems as if it is quite possible unless the companies involved are carefully regulated. Opponents argue that there is a very real risk of the practice threatening wildlife species and polluting waterways.

In March 2014, a report, *Are We Fit to Frack?*, was launched by a number of the UK's leading wildlife and countryside groups – including the Angling Trust, the National Trust, RSPB, the Salmon & Trout Association, The Wildlife Trusts and the Wildfowl & Wetlands Trust. In addition, it was supported by a cross-party group of MPs.

CLIMATE CHANGE

In July 2014, the Committee on Climate Change (CCC) claimed that, in general – and despite the previous winter's atrocious flooding in parts of the country – Britain is still not doing enough to tackle the risks from climate change. They also blamed intensive farming, local council inertia and the fact that funding set aside to deal with flood problems are being used elsewhere. The CCC maintained that three-quarters of existing flood defences are inadequately maintained because of a cash shortage – and that at the current rates of investment, flood risks for people in England will increase.

Rules to avoid floods affecting new developments have also been delayed.

In reply, the government stated that it had offered an extra £270 million to repair storm-damaged defences and was committed to adapting infrastructure to extreme weather – but Lord Krebs, chair of the CCC's adaptation sub-committee, told *BBC News*: 'The £270m announced by government is a one-off payment to repair damage – not to invest in the future… The Environment Agency shows that unless increased investment is sustained until the 2020s, the risk of flood damage will actually increase… If you don't maintain defences properly you will just stack up problems. We are calling on the government to be transparent and explain the rationale behind their policy.'

The report (based upon the document *Hydraulic Fracturing for Shale Gas in the UK: Examining the Evidence for Potential Environmental Impacts*) contained ten recommendations based on a technical evidence report reviewed by the Centre for Ecology and Hydrology, one of Britain's leading ecological research institutes – as a result of which various countryside groups requested that all protected wildlife areas, nature reserves and national parks be 'frack-free zones' due to the fact that a lack of regulation around shale gas exploitation could easily have a serious impact on a wide range of threatened species.

Of particular interest as far as we ditch-lovers are concerned is the possible impact of drilling and contamination on some of our most precious water-based natural habitats, particularly chalk streams which, apart from anything else – as pointed out in 'Men of the meadows' (page 8) – all form an integral part of ditch and drainage culture. At the time of the report's launch, Janina Gray, the Salmon & Trout Association's head of science, said: 'The water use of the UK shale gas industry could exacerbate pressure on rivers and wetlands, particularly on sensitive water bodies and those already suffering from over-abstraction, such as chalk streams, and this adds yet further pressure on declining fish populations… This, coupled with the risk of water pollution – including groundwater contamination – could, if not correctly managed, be significant – possibly irreversible. Action must be taken now to ensure all necessary environmental protection and regulatory frameworks are in place before extraction goes ahead.'

WHAT'S TO BE DONE?

Janina Gray of the Salmon & Trout Association was talking specifically about the possible effects of fracking when she said that 'Action must be taken now…' but her words apply equally well to many other aspects of countryside management and well-being. One of the biggest problems is the wholesale clearance of ditches, which is still common practice in many agricultural areas despite recent occurrences proving that a good, well-maintained network of ditches and other drainage methods is essential to prevent flooding.

DREDGING

Dredging rivers is not always the answer to preventing flooding: indeed, the very mention of the word causes much controversy. Conservation groups and others oppose the idea of widening and deepening rivers on the grounds that doing so results in ecological damage and simply results in flooding further downstream because of the increased water flow coming to an abrupt halt at some insurmountable bottle-neck. Dame Helen Ghosh, director-general of the National Trust, put it well when, in a *Country Life* article in February 2013, she pointed out: 'When rivers are "canalised", they run fast and "scour", dragging all the silt with them, which causes flooding', and cited examples of where, on National Trust property, projects were in hand to 'let the river return to meandering' or 'restore the old course of the river'.

A STITCH IN TIME

On the rivers and in the more major waterways, much work is being done – and whilst similar remedial activity may not be practicable or even desirable in the ditch or stream situation, such work is well worth a mention here.

In some quarters, rivers are deliberately altered so as to slow up the water flow in order that it meanders rather than gushes to a point where flooding might occur. In other situations, landowners and farmers are being encouraged to grow trees to take up some of the water before it reaches the ditch and also to slow water entering rivers.

Gently pushing parts of the riverbank into the water's edge will help re-grade what environmentalists call the 'bed-to-bank profile', whilst

A meandering ditch is, for a variety of reasons, far better environmentally than is one that runs straight and canal-like.

tipping quantities of gravel into the centre of a river has the obvious effect of raising the river bed. Un-straightening previous straight stretches of bank and creating islands in the centre of the wider rivers has the desired effect of altering the speed and direction of the water flow. Even something as simple as placing and securing a tree trunk in the water at a strategic point can be extremely beneficial.

Far less beneficial was the traditional practice of supporting the riverbank by means of sheet piling, and during the course of many recent projects these have been removed and replaced with hazel faggots. Although temporary, they do far more to support the rivers and flood plains – and they offer the possibility of homes and feeding areas for many forms of wildlife.

WELFARE PROSPECTS FOR WILDLIFE

Nature conservation in the British countryside is driven by a wide range of policies, legislation and agreements, all of which are delivered by a wide range of independent bodies from the statutory, voluntary, and academic and business sectors. When all is as it should be, these, in turn, work together in order to conserve both the environment and its biodiversity.

The Wildlife Trusts, for example, want to 'help nature to recover from the decline that for decades has been the staple diet of scientific studies and news stories' and, on their website, state that 'wildlife and natural processes need to have space to thrive, beyond designated nature reserves and other protected sites' and that to achieve this, 'it is vital that the richest wildlife sites are protected and sustained as a starting point from which nature can spread back into our wider landscapes'. There is, then, no better place to begin than with the humble yet incredibly environmentally important ditch and similar watercourses.

'The River, [I live] by it and with it and on it and in it… It's my world, and I don't want any other.' So remarked Ratty in Kenneth Grahame's *The Wind in the Willows*. 'Ratty' – aka the water vole – is making an encouraging comeback despite (as has already been seen in Chapter 3, page 55) almost becoming extinct in British ditches and similar places. While many water authorities have undertaken the repairs and necessary maintenance of the waterway banks for which they are responsible with the habitat of the water vole in mind, it is, however, the constant catching and culling of the American mink by landowners, farmers and gamekeepers which

The water vole is making an encouraging comeback due in no small part to the care and consideration of water authorities when carrying out repairs and necessary maintenance – and, of course, the concerted efforts of many wildlife groups. (Photo: Pedro/Wikimedia Commons)

has probably done most to help their numbers. The presence of mink is not always easy to detect and, if they did but know it, the current water vole population has much reason to be grateful to the Game and Wildlife Conservation Trust's (GWCT) invention of a 'mink raft'.

An interesting scenario

While a 'sparrow in a cage' apparently 'sets all Heaven in a rage', in 2014 it seemed that the possibility of a family of beavers, which had been living wild on the River Otter in Devonshire and were threatened with being caught and placed in a zoo or wildlife park, had caused some local residents and a national charity to get in a similar state.

Various wildlife groups and charities were against general government thinking – the essence of which was that the beavers were a non-native, invasive species that could be carrying disease and should therefore be removed from the riverbank and tested before being found a home in captivity.

Subsequent legal proceedings challenged the government's plans, claiming that because Britain was part of the beavers' natural range before they were hunted to extinction, they are protected under European law. As a compromise, the government said that it would test the beavers for disease

The GWCT Mink Raft encourages mink to leave evidence of their presence in the form of footprints and uses a standardised mixture of clay and sand to record the tracks over a period of one to two weeks. Once detected, the raft(s) on which the mink left its tracks also becomes the best place to set a trap.

Through a series of trials, the GWCT established that one raft per kilometre of waterway gave the best opportunities of detecting the whereabouts of mink and, in their research findings, observed that: 'Given more than one raft available per mink and successive check periods, there is only a very small risk of failing to detect a mink... With this knowledge, rafts can also be used as a reliable indicator of mink absence. That's very important, because the number of mink caught is a poor guide to the success of the control effort. It is the extent to which the [area] is clear of mink that matters.'

closer to their West Country home rather than 300 miles away in York as it had previously been intended. All seemed happy with this decision because that would make it easier for the animals to be re-released in Devon.

The Department for Environment, Food and Rural Affairs (Defra) gave sole responsibility for the potential re-release of the beavers to Natural England because, in 2009, Natural England had published a report that had extolled the benefits of releasing beavers back into the wild. The report said beavers could improve fish stocks and their dams could help prevent flooding by slowing down the flow of water from high ground. A pro campaigner and spokesman further commented: 'We're delighted that the government appears to be listening to local people who want these beavers to swim freely in their rivers... Beavers are a protected, native species, and testing them and re-releasing them into the wild would absolutely be the sensible thing to do. Allowing beavers to remain in the wild in England would bring major benefits – such as boosting fish stocks, improving our waterways and bringing a bit more happiness to our countryside.'

In January 2015, Natural England awarded the Devon Wildlife Trust a five-year licence to manage the beaver colony on a trial basis, but only after the animals had been checked to ensure that they were a 'native' European species and that they were free from the *Echinococcus multilocularis* parasite.

Not everyone was happy at this decision. Only time will tell whether the re-establishment of beavers onto UK waterways will prove to be a good or bad thing, and their activities help or hinder the problems of flooding. Ditches and similar waterways are extremely important aspects of an overall ecosystem, containing, as they do, all manner of plants and wildlife. When the natural balance is disturbed by non-indigenous, sometimes invasive species, it can have far-reaching effects.

BUFFER STRIPS

Buffer strips are in use in areas of farmland under Stewardship schemes and similar – and also along the banksides of some ditches and waterways. Their purpose is to protect sensitive areas from the effects of spray drift when chemicals such as pesticides have to be applied to agricultural farmland.

Some buffer strips are a legal requirement, especially when it comes to protecting aquatic life, while others are voluntary or based on recommendations made by one of the various advisory bodies. They might simply be a strip of existing land on which no spraying is done or they could consist of a grass crop planted specifically for the purpose of screening a waterway from any possible spray drift. Their width varies but should be at least six metres – and considerably more in situations where there is a more than 20 degree slope down to the water's edge. The 'Chlorpyrifos – say

Buffer strips are extremely important to all manner of wildlife, but particularly butterflies.

FLOODED FAUNA AND FLORA

Although already mentioned whenever directly appropriate to a particular plant, bird or beast, it is essential to consider whether, on a more general basis, the effects of recent flooding in many parts of the UK have had nothing but a detrimental influence on the native species.

Whilst undesirable, invasive plants such as Japanese knotweed and the like do, unfortunately, spread downstream in such events, but so too do more 'desirable' native plants whose seed are transported in flood water and colonise new areas quite successfully. Likewise, though water voles, for instance, can be flooded from their burrows, or even drown in rapidly rising flood water it can, for the survivors, aid their dispersal and result in a wider distribution of the species in the following breeding season.

For some, then, it has been a 'good thing'; for others, a catastrophe. After the winter floods of 2013/14, for example, a spokesperson for the British Dragonfly Society said: 'some [dragonfly] nymphs would survive by hanging onto vegetation or hiding in mud' but that 'the winter storms and huge waves will have driven saltwater into freshwater lakes and rivers near coasts, echoing the great 1953 flood which saw the dainty dragonfly driven to extinction in the UK'. She also noted that the dredging of rivers in Somerset was likely to be 'extremely damaging for the nymph'. (See also the notes on dredging earlier in this chapter.)

"No" to Drift' campaign, launched in 2012, recommends that farmers use a combination of low-drift nozzles on their sprayers plus a 20 metre wide spray-free buffer.

An incidental, but extremely important, additional benefit associated with buffer strips is that they can also help create the types of wildlife corridors mentioned on several previous occasions throughout this book.

PLANT FOR WILDLIFE

Repairing bankside damage caused by flooding can be nothing but beneficial for the environment in general and wildlife in particular. Trees washed out from the banksides should be replaced with, if not exactly the same species as has been lost, most certainly ones that are native to the vicinity. As to when they should be planted, I think as Zambian economist Dambisa Moyo did when she famously remarked: 'The best time to plant a tree is 20 years ago. The second best time is now.'

In most instances, and even after the most devastating flooding, wild plants usually manage to re-colonise of their own accord over a period of time. Sometimes, though, it may be necessary to consider the reintroduction of marginal plants. Such remedial work should, however, only ever be done after great consideration – and with a constant awareness of the long-term consequences of your actions. Introduction of plants to an area in which the species were not previously known is potentially detrimental to the local ecology and should be avoided at all costs.

At a glance

* Identify water margin plants growing in the immediate region – and plant only those of the same species.
* Check with the Environment Agency and/or your local Defra office regarding the legalities of plant reintroduction.
* Consider whether it might be viable to take roots or cuttings from places where there is a surfeit.
* Where such action is not possible, find out whether or not any remedial work is being done elsewhere in the area – surplus plants may become available as a result of routine ditch or stream maintenance.
* Before moving plants from one place to another, where practicably possible, it will pay to rinse off the roots (well away from natural watercourses) in order to reduce the risk of carrying unwanted parasites etc. to a new location.
* If your only option is to consider commercial plant suppliers, make every effort to seek out a specialist grower of British wild plants rather than a general garden centre – and always ask whether the details of origin are known.
* Never be tempted into introducing water margin plants more usually seen in a garden than in the wild – that is exactly how many unwanted, invasive species have become established in the British countryside.
* For more detailed help and advice, check out Flora locale (www.floralocale.org) – a charity established to promote the use of native flora for countryside restoration and other biodiversity projects.

RIPARIAN RESPONSIBILITIES

It has often been said that good drainage makes for good neighbours. Unfortunately, drainage of water is one of the most common areas of dispute

Sometimes it may be necessary to consider the reintroduction of marginal plants. Such remedial work should, however, only ever be done after great consideration.

between rural neighbours, whether they be farmers or not. Generally, if you live in or own property that is next to any watercourse (ditches included), or there's a watercourse that runs through your property, you are what is known as a 'riparian landowner' and have 'riparian rights'. Sometimes, such as when a prime trout river meanders through, this can be quite advantageous and beneficial to the keen fisherman or woman, but with the pleasures also comes responsibility.

If the ditch or waterway runs along the boundary of the property, it is likely that you will be in joint ownership with your neighbour and, unless the land registry deeds show differently, it is assumed that each own their side to the centre of the water – and are each responsible for their own bank maintenance and repair. In addition, it is the riparian owner's responsibility to clear any debris, natural or otherwise, from the water itself – even if it did not originate from their land.

SHIRKING RESPONSIBILITY

In the event of a riparian owner refusing to 'make good' any ditch which has fallen into disrepair and which may, in time, cause flooding or similar damage to surrounding land, the usual course of action is perhaps best explained in general terms by William Howarth writing in *Wisdom's Law of Watercourses* (5th edition, 1992):

> Where a ditch is in such condition as to cause
> injury to any land or to prevent the improvement

of drainage of any land, the Agricultural Lands
Tribunal* may... make an order requiring the
person or persons named in the order to carry
out work for cleansing the ditch, removing from
it any matter which impedes the flow of water,
or otherwise putting it in proper order, and for
protecting it as specified in the order. An order
with respect to a ditch may name any person who
is the owner or occupier of land through which
the ditch passes or which abuts on the ditch...

An order requiring remedial work to be carried
out on a ditch is sufficient authority for the
named person to do the work specified and, so far
as may be necessary for that purpose, to enter land
specified by the order. Where work specified in an
order has not been carried out after three months,
or any longer time specified in the order, the
appropriate Minister or a drainage body authorised
by him may carry out the work and enter any land
which it is necessary to enter for that purpose...

A person entitled to enter land by virtue of a
default order of this kind may take with him
other persons and equipment, but if the land is
unoccupied he must leave it as effectively secured
against trespassers as he found it.

*NB: In July 2013, the government abolished three of the key tribunals dealing with land matters – one of which was the Agricultural Lands Tribunal (ALT). Up until that time, the ALT dealt with matters such as termination of agricultural tenancies and succession – and also with a number of drainage disputes in relation to land. After July 2013, all three bodies became part of what is now referred to as the 'First Tier Tribunal'. In situations of appeal, instead of going to the High Court as was previously the case, the outcome is now determined by an 'Upper Tribunal'.

Your ditch or mine?

As with riparian responsibilities affecting an open ditch or stream, a ditch with a hedge running alongside may cause confusion (and dispute) as to who is responsible for what in the way of care and maintenance.

It is generally the riparian owner's responsibility to ensure that ditches and waterways on his land are kept clear of debris and free-flowing.

The age-old custom when digging a ditch on a boundary was to dig and then throw the spoil back onto your side; on which you'd subsequently plant a hedge. To all intents and purposes, the newly-dug ditch would then be in the neighbour's field. Unless any property deeds say otherwise, no matter

BASIC RIPARIAN OBLIGATIONS

* A riparian owner is responsible for accepting water from their upstream neighbour and transferring this, along with any additional drainage from their property, freely, to their downstream neighbour.
* You cannot obstruct, pollute or divert any flow of water that might affect the rights of others.
* Any flooding of your land caused by 'inadequate capacity downstream' has to be accepted – there is apparently no common law for a landowner to improve the drainage capacity of a watercourse, no matter how small.

A ditch with a hedge running along the top of a bank — as is the case here to the right — may cause confusion (and dispute) as to who is responsible for what in the way of care and maintenance.

how long ago the ditch was dug and the hedge planted, you do, however, still own to the far side of the ditch and have the right to go across to maintain it. Legal presumption defines it as follows:

> Where two properties are divided by a hedge (or bank) and a ditch, the boundary is presumed to be on the far side of the ditch from the hedge. This presumption is based on the surmise that the owner of the land, standing on his side of the boundary looking towards his own land, dug his drainage ditch within his own land and planted a hedge on the mound of earth removed from the ditch.

DITCH MAINTENANCE

If open ditches are not regularly maintained it is quite likely that vegetation growth will slow down any regular water flow and cause silting, as will any bank slippage or erosion. In the opinion of most, appropriate clearance and maintenance should, therefore, be carried out on a regular basis. Primrose McConnell's *The Agricultural Handbook* (first published in 1883 but with many subsequent and revised editions), has it that 'a reasonable interlude between ditch bottom cleaning is five years, with annual attention to the vegetation on the banks'. The time of year to do this is, of course, from the point of view of flora and fauna, absolutely crucial. Defra offer some valid, practical advice – amongst which is included the following:

* Clear ditches and dykes in the autumn or winter when conditions allow. Clearing in the spring or summer can be more problematic for breeding birds, plants and insects.
* Only working on one bank at a time and cutting/clearing different ditches in different years will minimise the impact on wildlife and benefit the environment in the long run.
* When cutting the bankside, try to leave 10–15 cm of vegetation to provide cover and food sources for animals such as water voles.

AN EXCEPTION TO THE RULE

The Agricultural Handbook reckons that the ditch bottom should be cleared every five years. Although maintaining the ditch as a whole might include 'annual attention to the vegetation on the banks' or, as Defra advise, 'only working one bank at a time… in different years', there are occasions when, in the interest of diversity, a longer period could possibly be more beneficial. By considering longer rotations of between five and eight years, both species which prefer clear, open sites and those that need choked, well-vegetated ditches will always have somewhere to thrive.

TO DIG OR NOT TO DIG

Clearing and cutting back is one thing, attempting to increase the depth of an existing ditch is another. Apart from possibly falling foul of any conditions of riparian ownership and responsibility, as efficient

Cutting and clearing alternate banks in different years will minimise the impact on wildlife – and benefit the environment in the long run.

and practical though digging deeper ditches might be in an attempt to reduce future flooding, The Wildlife Trusts' website (www.wildlifetrusts.org) points out that doing so 'will result in lower ground water levels throughout the rest of the year, which may affect a wide range of plant communities and the species that depend on them'.

There might well have been a ditch running through a particular area way back when, but that doesn't give anyone a natural automatic right to restore it if doing so means re-digging. Any such work might need the permission of the Environment Agency (in Scotland, the Scottish Environment Protection Agency).

CREATING A DITCH

In certain situations, one might be found guilty of breaking the law if you were to drain land considered essential wildlife habitat. In March 2014, a landowning farmer was fined for failing to maintain an important wildlife site in the Lake District. It was proven to the magistrate's satisfaction that the man had not complied with a land 'Remediation Notice', issued under the Environmental Impact Agriculture Regulations 2006* – a notice issued as a result of his installing a number of underground pipes on his land, with the result that water which should have been a part of the natural environment was drained into a river. At the time of the prosecution, Janette Ward, Natural England's regulation director, said: 'We are always disappointed by having to bring prosecutions, as it means that some of England's most important wildlife has been damaged. We hope that the affected area will now be able to recover as far as possible and look forward to working closely with [this particular landowner] so that the land can be returned to its original condition.'

*NB: The Environmental Impact Agriculture Regulations are in force to protect semi-natural areas of land such as heathland, wildflower-rich meadows and pasture, and land that has not been physically or chemically cultivated in the previous 15 years. Their aim is to protect the most environmentally significant land from agricultural intensification – and also guard against possible negative environmental effects from the physical restructuring of rural land holdings, such as changes to field boundaries. They do this by requiring landowners to seek approval from Natural England before carrying out any project that increases the productivity for agriculture of uncultivated land or semi-natural areas.

Replacing an existing open ditch with an alternative underground system of drainage pipes may result in the person responsible falling foul of the 2006 Environmental Impact Agriculture Regulations – particularly if the water is an integral part of the natural habitat.

CURVES, NOT ANGLES

In less sensitive situations – and bearing in mind all that has been written with regard to riparian ownership and responsibilities – it might well be possible to create a new ditch on your property. If you do, you'll be in good company as, at least according to Ranulph or Ralph Higden, a monk of Chester, writing circa 1350 about Edward II:

> *... from his youth he devoted himself in private to the art of rowing and driving carts, of digging ditches and thatching houses, as was commonly said, and also with his companions at night to various works of ingenuity and skill, and to other pointless trivial occupations unsuitable for the son of a king.*

Of royal descent or not, assuming an understanding of the legalities as mentioned above, a ditch should follow the lie of the land and maintain an adequate fall throughout its length, taking into account any steep gradients and natural obstructions. Ideally, it should not be straight, but instead include a gentle curve or two in order to slow down the flow of water – angles are, however, best avoided as water forcing its way past such points could result in unwanted bank erosion. Ensuring a variety of bankside profiles will also help in encouraging a greater diversity of wildlife species and, where possible, the shallower slopes should be in places which receive the most sunlight.

As to its dimensions, there are, given the exceptions for wildlife outlined above, certain general formulae set out with regards to height ´ width ´ depth, but in addition, various internet sites each independently suggest that a ditch should typically be:

> ... at least 300mm deep and 300mm wide at the base... chamfered and widening to approximately 500mm at the top [vertical sides may collapse with the weight of saturated ground above the ditch sides, or if water erodes the base and undercuts the sides] ... at least 500mm away from [any] path or hedge to avoid path collapse into the ditch.

HANDSOME IS AS HANDSOME DOES...

The whole point of a ditch is to serve a practical purpose – that of draining nearby land and keeping the subsequent water flowing – but it doesn't mean to say that, irrespective of whether or not it passes through a garden area or a chunk of countryside, it should be an eyesore and quite literal 'blot on the landscape'.

A ditch is, of course, just that and one cannot be created without digging out soil which then needs to be put somewhere. Forming a bank on which wildlife-friendly plants and shrubs can be planted at a later date is one way of preventing an eyesore – and is certainly cheaper than having the soil taken away in a lorry.

A meandering ditch is more pleasing than a straight one and will, as we have seen, be of more benefit in slowing water flow and preventing flooding further down the line. A curving ditch is also less likely to erode over time and is certainly far better when it comes to enhancing the prospects for water-loving flora and fauna.

WATER OUTLET PIPES

The water from permitted underground drainage pipes (see Environmental

With a few stones salvaged from nearby, an attractive
feature can be made of where an underground pipe
or overflow from a pond emerges into a ditch.

Impact Agriculture Regulations above) obviously has to go somewhere
– most likely into an open ditch or stream. These pipes will work just
as efficiently if they are simply exposed at their ends but can be made
an attractive feature with very little effort, a few stones salvaged from
the nearby fields and some cement. Making a stone surround also has a
practical purpose in that it helps prevent soil erosion from around the
pipe – which would otherwise undoubtedly happen over time.

IN CONCLUSION

At least the flooding of the last couple of winters has proved to one and
all the importance of ditches as a means of drainage. Hopefully they will,

from hereon in, be better maintained and cherished – and not just for crucial practical reasons, but equally because of their value in playing a vital and often unique role in the well-being of Britain's flora and fauna.

Then there is the pleasure given to the interested country lover who, armed with a little knowledge and a lot of enthusiasm, can spend many happy hours, eyes down, exploring a ditch and its environs or, if even that is too energetic, simply sitting on the bank watching the aquatic world go by.

> Beat out as I was and in need of a doze,
> I laid myself down where a grassy bank rose
> By the side of a ditch, in arboreal shade,
> Where I stretched out my feet, and pillowed my
> head...

(From *The Midnight Court* by Brian Merriman, 1749–1805)

SOURCES, BIBLIOGRAPHY AND FURTHER READING

Buckton, Henry: *Yesterday's Village Life*; David & Charles, 2005

Burton, Robert (and various contributors): *The Book of The Year – a natural history of Britain through the seasons*; Frederick Warne, in association with Books for Children, 1983

Carter, David: *Butterflies & Moths in Britain and Europe*; Pan Books, in association with William Heinemann and the British Museum (Natural History), 1982

Carter, Sam (compiler and editor): *Curious Observations – a country miscellany from the pages of* Country Life; Simon & Schuster, 2011

Culpeper, Nicholas: *Culpeper's Complete Herbal*; first published in 1653 but latterly by Arcturus Publishing, 2009

Facas, Michelle: *An Introduction to 19th Century Art*; Routledge, 2011

Grant Watson, E. L.: The *What to Look For...* series; Ladybird Books, 1959–1963

Haslam, Sylvia Mary; Wolseley, P. A.: *River Vegetation, Its Identification, Assessment and Management*; CUP Archive, 1981

Hobson, J C Jeremy: Cook Game; Crowood Press, 2008

Hobson, J C Jeremy: Curious Country Customs; David & Charles, 2007

Howarth, William: *Wisdom's Law of Watercourses (5th edition)*; Shaw & Sons, 1992

Humphreys, John (and various contributors): *Treasured Tales of the Countryside*; David & Charles, 2003

Jefferies, Richard: *Hodge and his Masters – round about a great estate*; first published in 1880, but with many reprints since

Louv, Richard: *Last Child in the Woods*; latest revised edition, Atlantic Books, 2010

Mabey, Richard: *Food for Free*; first published in 1972, new (pocket) edition Collins, 2012

Marriat-Ferguson, J. E.: *Visiting Home*; published privately, 1905

Matthews, W. H.: *Mazes and Labyrinths*; first published in 1922, new edition Dover Publications, 1970

McConnell, Primrose: *The Agricultural Handbook*; first published in 1883 but with many revised editions since

Moss, Stephen: *BBC The Great British Year – wildlife through the seasons*; Quercus, 2013

Moss, Stephen: *The Bumper Book of Nature*; Square Peg, 2009

Ransome, Arthur: *Pond and Stream*; Anthony Treherne & Co. Ltd, 1906

Reader's Digest: *Field Guide to the Animals of Britain*; 2nd, revised edition, 2001

Seymour, John: *The New Complete Book of Self-Sufficiency*; Dorling Kindersley, 2003

Silsby, Jill: *Dragonflies of the World*; Smithsonian, 2001

Sterry, Paul: *Collins Complete Guide to British Wild Flowers*; Collins, 2008

Sterry, Paul: *Collins Complete British Wildlife Photo-guide*; HarperCollins, 1997

Ure, David: *General View of the Agriculture in the County of Dumbarton*; 1794

Vermeulen, Heiko: *The Lightfoot Guide to Foraging – wild foods by the wayside*; EURL Pilgrimage Publications, 2012

Willoughby; Charles: *Come and Hunt*; Museum Press, 1952